The
Dog-Gone Good
Cookbook

The
Dog-Gone Good
Cookbook

100 Easy, Healthy Recipes for Dogs and Humans

Gayle Pruitt

Photographs by Joe Grisham

St. Martin's Griffin
New York

Photo credits: Joe Grisham, Photographer, and Janet Healey, Art Director

Dogs were provided by the following rescue organizations: Metroplex Mutts, Paws in the City, Coppell Humane Society, Poodle Rescue Center of North Texas, and Healing Species of Texas.

www.stmartins.com

Design by Susan Walsh

ISBN 978-1-250-01451-1 (trade paperback)
ISBN 978-1-250-02090-1 (e-book)

First Edition: February 2013

10 9 8 7 6 5 4 3 2 1

To Mimi and Casper,

my canine kids

Contents

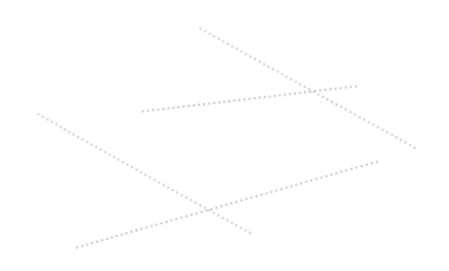

Acknowledgments

Without the wonderful Chancey Blackburn this book would never have been written. She helped me every step of the way. And thank you to the brilliant Linda Langton, my agent, for whom I have come to have the highest respect! Many thanks to Daniela Rapp, my editor. I also want to thank set directors V'Annie Turner and Janet Healey for their inspiration and work on three of the stunning photographs by Joe Grisham that caught the publisher's attention. And a big thank-you to set director, Keith Johnston.

—GAYLE PRUITT

First and foremost, I have to thank Janet Healey, my wife and a very talented art director. Her exceptional ideas and tireless pursuit of a beautiful photo is the secret to my success. She's the reason people look at my images and say WOW! Special thanks go to Keith Johnston for production design and styling. Your work is flawless, and you made this project a joy to shoot. Also, thanks to stylist V'Anne Paur-Turner for your amazing contribution. Much appreciation to TC Bombet and J.J. Leeds for dog wrangling. Not only were the models on their mark, but you did a great job of getting their ears up just when I needed it. To all the dogs and volunteers from Metroplex Mutts, Paws in the City, Coppell Humane Society, Poodle Rescue of North Texas, and Healing Species of Texas, thank you for the endless sit-stays and for allowing us to show the world how truly wonderful you are. Last, but certainly not least, thank you Bibi and Murphy, my favorite rescue dogs. You went to great lengths as fit models, stand-ins, and impromptu hosts. Your tolerance for regular visits from enemy dogs is to be applauded.

—JOE GRISHAM

RULES OF THE KITCHEN · OPEN DAILY · ALL GOOD DOGS
WELCOME · MIMI EATS FIRST, NO EXCEPTIONS EVER ·
NO BEGGING · NO STANDING ON THE TABLE NO MATTER
HOW TEMPTING · CHEW CHEW CHEW CHEW YOUR FOOD
LEAVE IT MEANS LEAVE IT · NO WHINING · EAT
YOUR VEGETABLES · NO COUNTER SURFING · NO
FIGHTING, PUSHING OR SHOVING, THERE IS PLENTY
FOR EVERYONE · CATS AT OWN RISK · ANYONE
CAUGHT GOING THRU THE TRASH AFTER I HAVE
FIXED A PERFECTLY GOOD DINNER, WILL FORFEIT
TREATS FOR A WEEK · NO RUNNING, JUMPING
OR LOUD BARKING · WHAT'S ON MY
PLATE IS NONE OF YOUR BUSINESS · DROOLING
OK · WHAT HAPPENS IN THE KITCHEN STAYS
IN THE KITCHEN · NO HOWLING · TAKE
YOUR DAILY VITAMINS · NO CHASING
CASPER · NO WHINING · EAT THAT
PLATE FIRST · AGE BEFORE BEAUTY ·
PRETTY OR NO TREATS ·

Foreword

You are what you eat, and the same is true for your pets. At Paws & Claws Animal Hospital, my holistic veterinary hospital in Plano, Texas, the foundation of every health-care plan starts with a good natural diet. This is true whether the pet is sick and trying to recover from its illness, or the pet just needs to stay healthy in order to reduce the chance of developing serious diseases later in life.

As Gayle Pruitt states in her new book, *The Dog-Gone Good Cookbook,* cooking for your pet should be fun and easy as well as provide a nutritious diet for you and your pet. Included in the book are over 100 balanced, delicious recipes that are gluten-, corn-, and soy-free, in an effort to minimize any food reactions and maximize health.

Gayle has taken all the work out of cooking for your pet, as the book provides lists of foods that dogs should never have, lists of foods that you and your pet can experience together, as well as sections for equipment and supplies, techniques, staples and ingredients to keep on hand, and natural doggie supplements. The book also contains recipes for your "dog only" that are both raw and cooked.

Keeping with my theme of always trying to place my patients on the most natural and organic foods possible, all of these recipes suggest using organic and grass-fed foods whenever possible.

I know you will find *The Dog-Gone Good Cookbook* both user-friendly as well as a valuable resource for sharing a hearty meal with all of your family members, including the four-legged ones!

—SHAWN MESSONNIER, D.V.M. Author of the award-winning *The Natural Health Bible for Dogs & Cats* and *Unexpected Miracles: Hope and Holistic Healing for Pets,* and host of *Dr. Shawn: The Natural Vet,* on Martha Stewart Radio SiriusXM Channel 110

Introduction

I love to cook, but like most people, cooking for just me is not as much fun as cooking for others. There's nothing as fulfilling as sitting down and enjoying good, home-cooked food in the companionship of your family and friends. And if your BFF is your precious dog, my hope is that *The Dog-Gone Good Cookbook* will be your new constant cooking companion. *The Dog-Gone Good Cookbook* offers more than 100 delicious, healthy recipes that are wonderfully nutritious for both humans *and* canines.

I have two naughty little mutts, Mimi and Casper. When I first adopted my canine kids, their health was less than optimal. Mimi, a Dachshund/Chihuahua/Whatever mix, was a stray plucked off the streets of Dallas. A natural-born thief, she survived by eating out of garbage cans. She was nervous and had digestive issues. Casper, a Dachshund/Sweetheart mix, had been exposed to extreme stress and his hair was coming out in handfuls.

My background in nutrition gave me the knowledge that I needed to bring these little dogs back to full health by feeding them high-quality human-grade food with natural live nutrients. The end result has been amazing. Now these two little guys are happy and healthy.

I'm a certified nutritionist and chef. In my day job, I do nutritional research and develop recipes for businesses and food companies. I have also been reading and doing research on the ingredients in commercial dog foods, some of which I was buying and feeding to my furry babies. Considering what I learned about the less-than-desirable ingredients contained in these foods, I made the decision to cook for myself and my canine kids, using recipes that are delicious, yet nutritionally balanced as well as corn-, sugar-, soy-, and dairy-free. This has turned out to be the best decision I ever made. Not only has *their* health and well-being improved 100 percent, but so has *mine*. Being able to "cook healthy" for my dogs has given me more of an incentive to "cook healthy" for myself.

It has taken me several years to build up the courage to completely shuck commercial dog food. Like so many of us, I had been brainwashed into believing what the dog-food companies were saying. They stressed the importance of not feeding human food to dogs, because the dogs would not be getting all the nutrients they needed and it would cause imbalances and disease. A widely held myth has been that dogs will get fat if fed human food and would beg at the table. NOT TRUE!

Furthermore, I didn't question the ingredients in commercial dog food closely enough, until the scandal exploded about China dog- and cat-food manufacturers using melamine as filler. After in-depth research, I no longer believe labels when they describe their food as "all natural." Many contain sugar, artificial colors, preservatives—you get the picture.

After a little more research, I realized that for thousands of years dogs had been living with humans and eating human food. It wasn't until the 1900s that companies saw the potential for big money and started manufacturing food especially for dogs.

By looking into the practices of certain commercial dog-food companies, my mind was made up. I could certainly do a better job of providing nutrition to my two dogs by preparing their food myself. And I did.

However, at times it is impractical to make all your pet's food from scratch, so if you're feeding a good commercial-brand dog food and want to introduce some fresh, raw, or lightly cooked vegetables into your furry baby's diet, there is a section called "Sauces" just for you.

Today, Casper loves his food and savors every bite like a true gourmand. Mimi is not into haute cuisine; she enjoys her food but still swallows it whole. And Mimi and Casper have personally critiqued each of the recipes in *The Dog-Gone Good Cookbook* and give their tail-waggin' paws-up approval!

The changes have been amazing. Their noses are moist and soft. Their eyes are clear and sparkly. Their coats are shiny and their bodies are muscled and sleek. And their annual check-ups are perfect. They don't always mind me and they still can find ways to get in trouble, but I'm in heaven.

Dog owners who are taking care to monitor their own nutritional needs need to be advised of the same type of needs that guide their pets to vigor and good health. I wanted to write this book so that dogs can enjoy the maximum health for the longest life.

Fortunately for our beloved pets, awareness of and concern about the questionable contents of dry and wet commercial dog food has been growing in recent years. *The Dog-Gone Good Cookbook* provides dog owners an important alternative to purchasing these foods: home-cooked meals for your dogs that are delicious, nutritionally balanced and healthy, easy to prepare, and good for humans, too!

As you become familiar with my recipes and find more and more favorites, I hope you and your dog will enjoy better health, and that you will find friends with dogs to share *The Dog-Gone Good Cookbook*.

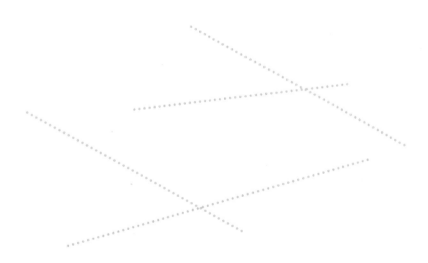

How to Use
The Dog-Gone Good Cookbook

I have been conducting nutritional research for humans since 1996, focusing some of my research on canine nutrition in recent years. Dog-food companies tell us that dogs should not eat "human" food.

While there are valid reasons such as weight control, nutritional balance, and toxicity, which would tell us to avoid *certain* human foods, my research has indicated that preparing meals for my two little rescues, Mimi and Casper, using fresh ingredients and lightly cooked *human*-grade foods, has enabled them to thrive.

There is no gluten, corn, or soy in the ingredient lists in *The Dog-Gone Good Cookbook*. Dairy is in only four recipes. I use organic, raw coconut oil, coconut flour, coconut milk, and shredded coconut for many of my recipes. Not only do the coconut products taste delicious, but coconut oil (and my recipes!) is also good for *people* with heart disease, diabetes, gluten intolerance, and for normalizing weight. As an added bonus, the recipes are easy to make!

All dogs, like people, are unique in looks, likes, personality, and in what is good for them. This book addresses general tastes for healthy dogs of all ages. Always check with your veterinarian to see if the recipes in this book have the right balance and the right ingredients for your particular pooch.

The recipes for your dog in the Human and Canine categories can be used along with a really good dog food that your veterinarian recommends on special occasions and in small amounts.

The *cooked* recipes in the Canines-Only category have anywhere between 35 to 42 percent protein, 40 to 48 percent carbohydrates, and 15 to 20 percent fat. All recipes in the Canine-Only category are high in omega-3 fatty acids. If you need to lower the carbohydrate content, you can always decrease the amount of rice or quinoa.

I also give my dogs a multivitamin, digestive enzymes, probiotics, and coconut and fish oils. Check the back of this book for a list of supplements and consult with your veterinarian regarding dosage.

Follow the guidelines in *The Dog-Gone Good Cookbook* and your dog will love you for it!

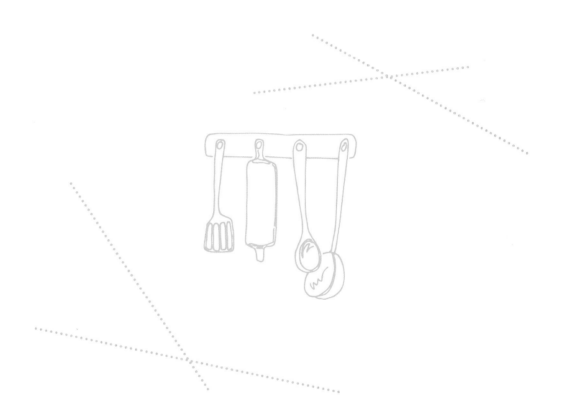

Equipment

There are four things you have to have to be able to cook and enjoy it:

1. The desire
2. The equipment
3. The right ingredients
4. The knowledge

This book can help with the equipment, the ingredients, and the knowledge. The desire has to come from you.

The equipment part is easy and important. If you're going to cook, even for Rover, you need the right equipment. Start off by making sure you have:

1. A couple of fairly large stainless-steel, glass, or ceramic bowls. (I'm not too fond of plastic.)
2. A large mixing spoon
3. Either a food processor or a powerful blender. (I use the food processor every day.)
4. A chef's knife, 8 or 9 inches long
5. Stainless-steel, glass, or ceramic cookware
6. A large stockpot
7. A nonstick nontoxic ovenproof skillet. (There are several brands now that are eco-friendly and some that are very inexpensive, so if possible, buy two—a large and a small.)

Staples

How many times have you wanted to cook from a recipe and ended up having to go to the store for several items, and then still didn't have everything? This section should help. Staples to always have on hand include:

1. Flax or chia seeds (preferably sprouted), kept in the refrigerator
2. Raw pumpkin seeds (may be called *Pepitas* in Spanish)
3. Canned pumpkin (not the pie filling!)
4. Eggs—pasture fed is best (more about that in the Supplements chapter)
5. Canned sardines in water
6. Bags of frozen peas, carrots, cauliflower, broccoli, and cranberries
7. Millet
8. Quinoa and quinoa flour
9. Coconut milk
10. Coconut flour
11. Coconut oil
12. Extra-virgin olive oil
13. Herbs (turmeric, fennel seeds, ground ginger, dill, sage, and many others; however, avoid onions and chives and use garlic sparingly)
14. Freezer-proof individual containers large enough for 2 or 3 meals per dog. There are several eco-friendly, reusable brands now.

Your Dog's Digestion and Oral Care

....

Your dog has a short digestive system, so it only takes about 8 to 9 hours for food to go from teeth and tongue to tail.

But before his food goes into his hungry little mouth, he has to smell it and he must like the smell. Dogs can outsniff you a million to one. No kidding, a dog literally has between 120 million to more than a whopping 220 million scent cells, depending on the breed. As mere humans, we have only about 5 million scent cells. And these canine supersniffers can store smells in their brains like we store data on a computer. Their heightened sense of smell helps with their sense of taste. Our canine buddies have only about 1,700 taste buds on their tongues, while we humans have about 9,000.

Dogs can taste sweet, salty, sour, and bitter. It seems the stronger the smell, the better they like it. Commercial dog-food companies have understood this, and have taken advantage by spraying fat smells and smoky scents directly onto kibbles, tricking dogs and dog parents. (If you knew what some of these kibbles were made from, you probably would not buy them for your pet and, without the fat smell and added scents, your dog probably would not eat them.)

So if you have to use commercial dog food by all means check the ingredient list.

A few examples:

- Nonhuman grade "meat by-products" may have little meat. These are the leftovers of any dead animal. "Meat by-products" might consist of organs not suitable for human consumption. They may also include blood, intestines, heads, feet, and feathers or possibly some dead, diseased animal.

- When "animal fat" is mentioned in the ingredient list, the fat could be from rendered animal fat, grease from a restaurant, or other rancid oils. Make sure that the ingredients list which animal is in the animal fat, such as "chicken fat" or "beef fat."
- "Food dye" should be avoided. Some artificial dyes are known carcinogens and may trigger an allergic reaction.

Unlike humans, who savor a good steak by chewing it thoroughly, dogs think if it smells good, it tastes good, and they will tear it apart and swallow it in as few bites as possible. Canine enzymes and strong stomach acids digest raw chunks of meat and bones in the stomach. The food becomes chyme, almost liquid, and then passes into the small intestine where the food is broken down even further. It can now be absorbed into the intestine wall and into the bloodstream, feeding vital nutrients to the body.

When the chyme finally arrives in the large intestine, most of the nutrients have been digested and absorbed so the remaining waste can be eliminated.

Bowwow! We finally got through that bit of education.

And before we get to the really fun stuff like how to make a delicious dinner for the whole family, *including* Fido, let's tackle one more lesson. This one is about canine oral care.

Plaque is a sticky, colorless film of bacteria that forms on teeth daily. It is the main cause of cavities and gum disease, and can harden into **tartar** if not removed each day.

Because tartar buildup bonds strongly to enamel, it can only be removed by a dental professional.

Gingivitis is the inflammation of the gum tissue often caused by tartar.

Mostly, it's carbohydrates that cause plaque and feed bacteria, which remain on the teeth after eating.

Having your dog's teeth cleaned at the veterinarian's often requires them to be put to sleep and given antibiotics. Having anesthesia is as risky for our dogs as it is for us. The use of antibiotics can kill the friendly bacteria that helps keep our dogs healthy. When antibiotics are recommended, use probiotics to replenish these good bacteria. (See Supplements chapter.)

In some cases this procedure is necessary, but there are a few things we can do to help prevent plaque buildup, to keep our dog's teeth pearly white, and to keep them out of the vet's office.

By all means, brush their teeth! You can buy little finger brushes to tackle this, and there are some good-tasting doggie toothpastes available so your sweet little furry friend won't take your finger off.

Also important—feed your dog good, human-grade food, and avoid corn or grain fillers. Use an enzyme in their water, which will prevent plaque buildup. (See Supplements chapter.) There are also some wonderfully effective dental chews on the market.

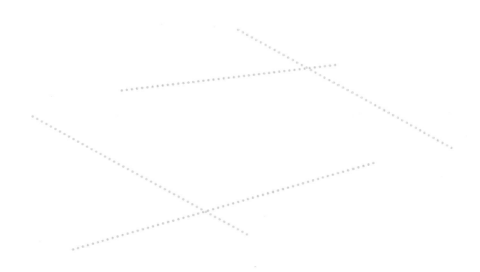

Foods That Are Toxic and Poisonous for Canines

Leave these foods off your "canine kids" diet!

1. Alcoholic beverages—can cause coma and even death.
2. Artificial sweeteners and *possibly* the herb stevia—may lower blood pressure.
3. Avocados—fruit, pits, and leaves—could cause fluid buildup in the lungs and chest.
4. Salmon; any raw fish.
5. Bones from fish and poultry—could cause lacerations in the digestive system.
6. Caffeinated beverages such as coffee and hot chocolate contain theobromine—can cause severe stimulation and may cause death.
7. Grapes (raisins)—could damage the kidneys.
8. Human vitamins—certain ingredients could be toxic. Check with your veterinarian.
9. Large amounts of liver—too much vitamin A can be toxic.
10. Macadamia nuts—could adversely affect numerous systems in the body.
11. Mushrooms—different mushrooms could cause shock or even death.
12. Nutmeg—could cause seizures and death.
13. Onions—raw, cooked, and powdered—could cause anemia.
14. Garlic in large amounts—can be toxic so use sparingly.
15. Spoiled food and foods that have started to decay—could contain many toxins.
16. Tomato leaves and stems—contains atropine that can cause tremors and heart arrhythmias.
17. Potatoes—contain properties that could cause tremors, seizures, and heart palpitations.

18. Rosemary—should be avoided if your dog has a history of seizures.
19. Salt—use sparingly.
20. Milk and other dairy products—for some dogs, could cause gas and bloating.

Animal Poison Control Center

If you think that your pet may have ingested a potentially poisonous substance, call (888) 426-4435. You can call for any animal poison-related emergency, 24 hours a day, 365 days a year. A $65 consultation fee may be applied to your credit card. For more information, visit www.aspca.org/pet-care/poison-control.

Why You Need to Feed Fruits and Vegetables to Your Dog

According to the 2005 Perdue Cancer Center studies of invasive urinary bladder cancer (invasive urothelial carcinoma or InvUC) in dogs, ". . . dogs experienced a reduction in InvUC risk, attributable to ingestion of vegetables. In fact, dogs in the study who consumed vegetables at least three times per week had a 70-percent reduction in bladder cancer risk."

The vegetables credited with the most reduction in InvUC were yellow and orange vegetables such as yellow or acorn squash, carrots or sweet potatoes. One wonders how many other cancers could be reduced by adding just a few fruits and vegetables to a canine's diet.

Why buy organic? Organic fruits and vegetables contain more antioxidants and more available nutrients. They also have much less harmful pesticides. Pesticides may cause allergic reactions and may also have dangerous estrogens that may weaken your immune system. Rinsing may not eliminate pesticides. Peeling may help but you will be losing many important vitamins and minerals. The best policy is to buy organic whenever possible.

Vegetables come in a delicious rainbow of colors. Each pigment has a task in the body. According to the *Old Farmer's Almanac*:

- GREEN Chlorophyll—All green vegetables contain chlorophyll, which may help disarm many carcinogens. Examples are kale, collard greens, broccoli, lettuces, and green beans.
- RED, ORANGE, YELLOW Carotenoids—Red, orange, and yellow vegetables may help protect the immune system and skin and could help prevent heart disease, and in some cases, macular degeneration. Some examples are tomatoes, red bell peppers, butternut squash, pumpkin, and yellow summer squash.
- BURGUNDY, PURPLE, BLUE Anthocyanins—May prevent, or even reverse age-related cognitive declines and neuro-degenerative diseases; also may improve night vision and other vision disorders, protect against heart disease, insulin resistance, and cancer, and promote wound healing. Examples are beets, red chard, blueberries, raspberries, and eggplant.

GOOD VEGGIES

Alfalfa sprouts (small amount)
Asparagus
Beets
Bell pepper (all colors)
Broccoli
Cabbage
Carrots
Cauliflower
Collards
Fennel
Green beans (lightly cooked)
Green peas

Kale
Lettuces (not iceberg, it's hard
    to digest and has very little
    nutritional value)
Snow peas
Spinach
Summer squash (yellow
    and zucchini)
Sweet potatoes
Winter squash (including acorn
    and pumpkin)

GOOD FRUITS

Apples (*without* seeds)
Bananas
Berries (fresh, frozen, or dried
    without sugar): blueberries,
    blackberries, strawberries,
    raspberries, etc.

Coconut (fresh, shredded
    unsweetened, coconut milk,
    etc.)
Melons

Basic Techniques

In this chapter, I explain how to brine, roast, and poach chicken and beef. I recommend filtered water for all of these recipes; in fact, I recommend using filtered water anytime you cook. There are directions for making chicken broth, and how to cook a beef roast and make beef broth. I explain how to make homemade vegetable broth, how to cook a pumpkin, and other handy ideas. There are also easy ways to cook rice and quinoa ahead of time for freezing in individual servings. Just triple the ingredients. That way, you avoid stress and save time when your schedule is crazy.

Brined Chicken

....

If you have never eaten chicken that has been brined, then you are in for a treat. Not only does brining draw out toxins from the chicken, but the brine is absorbed into the tissues, making the chicken juicer and more tender. The general rule is ¼ cup kosher salt per 1 quart of water.

Ingredients

    4 quarts water

    1 cup kosher salt

    1 whole chicken, rinsed

    Herbs of choice (I like a teaspoon of turmeric, thyme, dill, etc.)

In a large pot, combine enough water with kosher salt to cover chicken; stir. Place the whole rinsed chicken in the pot and add herbs. Cover and place in refrigerator for at least 6 hours or overnight.

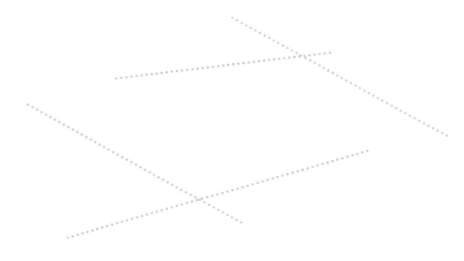

   Gayle Pruitt

Best Roast Chicken

Ingredients

    1 (3- to 4-pound) whole brined chicken (See recipe on page 22.)

    1 tablespoon olive oil

    Herbs of choice

Preheat oven to 325 degrees. Rinse chicken thoroughly. Then massage chicken with oil and herbs until covered. Place chicken in a glass or ceramic casserole dish, breast side down, and cook in oven for 30 minutes. Turn the chicken so breast side is up, cover loosely with aluminum foil, and cook another hour. Remove foil and continue cooking until chicken is crispy on top, about 30 minutes. Remove from oven and check for doneness; juices should run clear. Let stand about 15 minutes before carving.

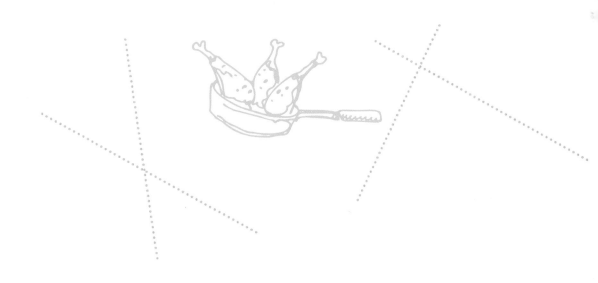

Best Poached Chicken & Chicken Broth for Dogs

Ingredients

1 (2-pound) whole chicken

Herbs of choice

3 to 4 carrots

3 stalks of celery

2 bay leaves

Brine a chicken. (See recipe on page 22.) Remove chicken from the brine and rinse thoroughly inside and out.

Place chicken in large pot, adding any herbs you like (but not garlic or onion powder!) and the remining ingredients. Fill pot with water 2 inches above the top of the chicken, cover. Bring water to a boil over high heat, then turn the burner to low and let simmer for 1 hour or until chicken is easily pulled apart. Remove chicken and let cool.

Continue simmering the broth for an additional hour. Remove bay leaves.

Braised Whole Chicken

Ingredients

    2 tablespoons olive oil

    1 (2-pound) whole chicken

    4 medium zucchini, ends removed, sliced into coins

    2 yellow squash, sliced into coins

    2 carrots, peeled and chopped

    1 green pepper, chopped

    1 stalk of celery, finely minced

    1 (10-ounce) can of tomato sauce

    1 teaspoon oregano

    Dash of Celtic sea salt

Add oil to a large heavy-bottomed pot and set burner to medium-high. Add chicken and sauté until brown. Add the rest of the ingredients. Cook on low heat, covered, for about 45 minutes or until chicken meat comes off the bone.

Boney Chicken or Turkey Carcass Broth

Ingredients

    2 chicken carcasses or 1 turkey carcass, reserved and frozen from a prior meal

    3 quarts water

    2 tablespoons Bragg Apple Cider Vinegar

    3 carrots, washed and coarsely chopped

    2 celery stalks, coarsely chopped

Add carcass, water, and vinegar to a large pot and let sit for at least 1 hour. Add the remaining ingredients, place on burner, and bring to a boil. Reduce heat and simmer for 3 hours.

The vinegar pulls the calcium out of the bones and into the broth.

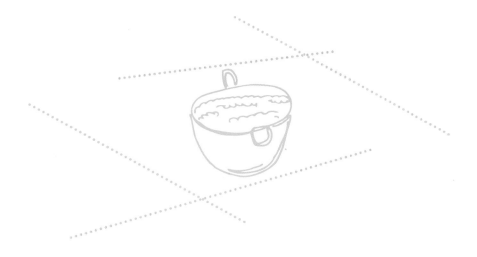

Best Beef Roast

Ingredients

  3 pounds chuck roast

  1 tablespoon herbs of your choice

  1 tablespoon olive oil

  Pinch of sea salt

  4 medium carrots, sliced into ¼-inch coins

Rub roast with herbs, oil, and salt. Place in a bowl, cover, and place in the refrigerator overnight.

Preheat oven to 300 degrees. Place roast in medium-size glass or ceramic lidded casserole dish, arranging the sliced carrots around roast. The roast and carrots should take up all the space in the casserole dish. Cover and bake in oven for about 3 to 3½ hours. Remove from oven and let rest 30 minutes before slicing. Slice against the grain for a more tender roast.

Reserve liquid for use in making doggie beef broth.

Boney Beef Broth

Ingredients

  5 pounds beef marrow bones (usually found in meat section of the grocery store freezer)

  3 quarts water

  2 tablespoons Bragg Apple Cider Vinegar

  3 carrots, washed and coarsely chopped

  2 stalks celery, coarsely chopped

Add bones, water, and vinegar to a large pot and let sit for at least 1 hour. Add remaining ingredients, place on burner over high heat, and bring to a boil. Reduce heat and simmer, uncovered, for 3 hours.

The vinegar pulls the calcium out of the bones and into the broth.

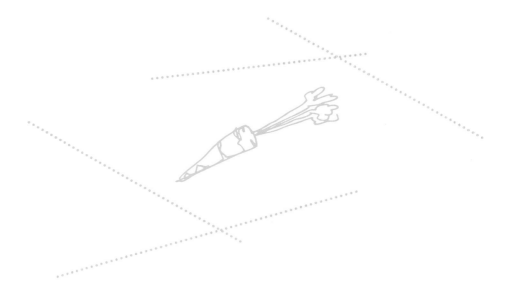

Meaty Beef Broth

Ingredients

- 5 pounds beef marrow bones (usually found in the meat section of grocery store freezer)
- ½ pound stew meat
- Reserved liquid from a roast (optional)
- ½ pound carrots, coarsely chopped
- 2 tablespoons coconut oil, melted
- 2 to 3 stalks of celery, coarsely chopped
- 1 to 2 green peppers, chopped (optional)
- 3 bay leaves

Preheat oven to 400 degrees. On a large baking sheet, place bones, stew meat, reserved liquid if using, carrots, and oil, and bake uncovered for about 35 minutes, until the meat starts to brown. Transfer the bones, meat, and carrots into a large 16-quart stockpot. Place the baking sheet on a burner and deglaze with a cup of water. Scrape all the brown bits and pour into the stockpot.

Fill the stockpot with cold water, 2 inches over the top of the bones. Add the remaining ingredients. Cook over high heat until the liquid starts to boil. Reduce heat, cover pot, and simmer for about 5 hours. Let the broth cool, then strain it, discarding the bones and vegetables, leaving only the broth. After the broth has cooled completely, freeze in individual freezer bags or containers.

Good idea: Name and date each bag with a marker or a label.

Homemade Vegetable Broth

Ingredients

    3 quarts water

    2 carrots, washed and coarsely chopped

    3 stalks of celery, coarsely chopped

    1 bell pepper, any color, coarsely chopped

    4 medium zucchini or yellow squash, coarsely chopped

    ½ cup parsley, loosely packed, chopped

    2 fresh bay leaves

    1 teaspoon thyme (or any other favorite herb)

Add all ingredients to a large pot and cook for 3 hours on medium-low heat. Strain broth and let cool, then discard vegetables. You may want to freeze in small servings.

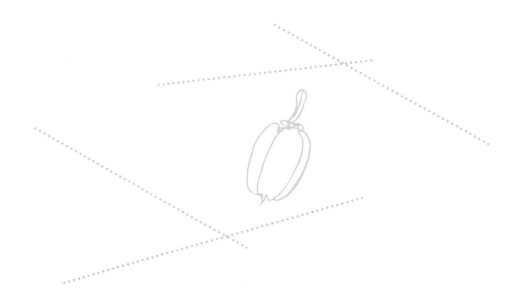

Baking a Pumpkin

Baked pumpkin can be used with so many dishes, such as a savory pumpkin soup, or just served as a side dish with some herbs and a little oil.

Wash a small or medium-sized whole pumpkin and place it on a foil-lined cookie sheet in a 350-degree preheated oven for about an hour. Check on the pumpkin after about 45 minutes by pressing on it with your thumb. If it gives, it's done. Remove from stove and cut off the top; let the pumkin sit until it cools. (Cutting off the top helps it cool down more quickly.)

With a spoon, scrape out the inside of the pumpkin and take out the seeds. (Do not throw away the seeds; they can be frozen and used in dog food.)

Cooking Brown Rice, Quinoa, and Millet

Here is some basic information for cooking brown rice, quinoa, and millet to serve to your canine.

When cooking rice, quinoa, or millet, the general rule is 1 part rice, quinoa, or millet to 2 parts liquid. However, for better digestion for canines, I have adjusted the normal ratios.

For rice, use 1 part rice to 2½ parts liquid. For quinoa or millet, use 1 part to 2¼ parts liquid. Also, cook an additional 10 minutes more than what the recipe calls for.

Brown Rice

....

Ingredients

    1 tablespoon olive oil

    1 cup brown rice

    2½ cups of water or other liquid

In a large pot, add oil and turn burner to medium. Add rice and stir, coating all grains with oil. Add the liquid and let it come almost to a boil before turning burner to low. Cover and cook for 45 minutes to an hour until the liquid has evaporated.

Quinoa

....

Ingredients

    1 tablespoon olive oil

    1 cup quinoa

    2¼ cups of water

In a large pot, add oil and turn burner to medium. Add quinoa; stir, coating all grains with oil. Add liquid and let it almost come to a boil before turning burner to low. Cover and cook for 30 to 35 minutes until the liquid has evaporated.

Millet

Ingredients

    1 tablespoon olive oil
    1 cup millet
    2¼ cups of water

In a large pot, add oil and turn burner to medium. Add millet and stir, coating all grains with oil. Add liquid and let it almost come to a boil before turning burner to low. Cover and cook for 30 to 35 minutes until the liquid has evaporated.

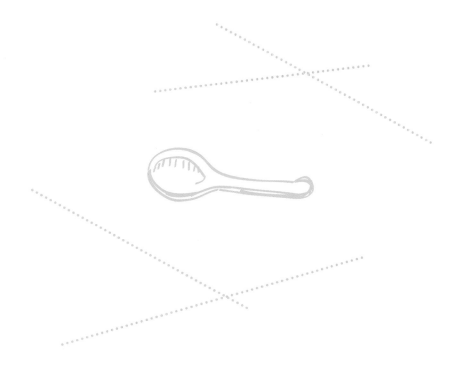

Human/Canine Entrées

~~~

These recipes are to be enjoyed by humans and dogs. They include soups and stews, beef, chicken, lamb, fish, and egg entrées. There are even recipes for the vegetarian family. Recipes are for the everyday meal, holidays, and when company comes. Let your meals cool to room temperature before serving to your dog. Yields are for human servings. Each dog's serving will depend on his size, breed, and metabolism.

Soups

Classic Chicken Soup

Ingredients

    1 (3–4 pound) whole chicken

    2 quarts water

    ½ pound carrots, washed and chopped coarsely

    ½ pound carrots, peeled and sliced about an inch on the bias

    3 stalks celery, chopped coarsely

    2 stalks celery, stringed and sliced on the bias

    2 bay leaves

    Dash of Celtic sea salt

    ¼ cup parsley, finely chopped

Wash the chicken and place it in a large pot with water, chopped carrots, chopped celery, bay leaves, and salt. Place on medium-high heat, cover, and cook for about 45 minutes or until the chicken starts coming off the bone. Remove chicken and place on a platter to cool. Cook the broth another 30 to 40 minutes.

Remove chicken meat from bone. Strain the broth and return it to the pot. Add the sliced carrots and sliced celery. Cook over medium-low heat until you can easily put a fork through the carrots.

Add the chicken meat back to the pot, add the finely chopped parsley, and cook for an additional 5 minutes before serving.

This soup freezes well.

Vegetarian Tomato Soup

Ingredients

- 1 red bell pepper, coarsely chopped
- 3 large carrots, peeled and sliced
- 1 tablespoon extra-virgin olive oil
- 1 cup red lentils, rinsed well
- 1 sweet potato, peeled and cut in 1-inch cubes
- 3 cups carrot juice (I buy bottled to save time)
- 2 cups water
- Dash of Celtic sea salt
- 1 (15-ounce) can tomato sauce
- 3 to 4 fresh basil leaves

In a large skillet, lightly sauté red peppers and carrots in oil for about 4 to 5 minutes. Add lentils, sweet potato, juice, and water, then cook for another 10 minutes. Add the salt and tomato sauce and cook an additional 10 minutes or until the lentils and sweet potato are soft. Add the fresh basil. Let the soup sit for a few minutes before serving.

Serves 6

Serve with brown rice to make a completely balanced protein meal. For a creamy starter soup, purée the soup in a food processor until it has a satinlike texture.

Gayle Pruitt

Braised Turkey Soup

Ingredients

    1 tablespoon coconut oil

    2 large turkey thighs

    Pinch of turmeric

    Pinch of Celtic sea salt

    Pinch of dried sage

    2 large carrots, chopped

    4 cups chicken broth (onion free; see recipes, pages 24, 27)

    2 roasted red peppers, sliced lengthwise (roast them or buy in a jar)

    ½ cup thinly sliced carrots

    ½ cup small cauliflower florets

    ½ cup snow peas

    ½ cup green frozen peas, thawed

Warm a heavy-bottom pot over medium-high heat; add coconut oil and turkey thighs skin side down. Cook until skin is golden brown. Turn and add turmeric, salt, dried sage, chopped carrots, and chicken broth. Simmer on low for about 40 minutes.

Remove turkey from pot and cut turkey meat off bone. Add turkey meat back to liquid and add roasted red pepper, sliced carrots, and cauliflower. Cook for another 10 minutes. Add snow peas and cook for an additional 3 minutes. Add green peas just before serving.

Serves 4

Red Rice and Red Lentil Soup

....

Ingredients

   2 quarts vegetable broth (onion free; see recipe, page 32)

   ½ cup red rice

   ½ cup red lentils, rinsed

   1 fennel bulb, chopped

   1 tablespoon olive oil

   ½ cup chopped carrots

   1 teaspoon thyme

   Celtic sea salt to taste

   ½ cup frozen peas

   4 to 5 fresh basil leaves

Add all ingredients except the peas and fresh basil to a 3- or 4-quart pot; cook on medium-low heat for about 45 minutes or until rice is done. Add frozen peas and the fresh basil and let sit for about 5 minutes.

Serves 8

Beef
Entrées

Beef Stew

Ingredients

- 1½ to 2 pounds chuck roast, cut in 2-inch cubes
- 2 tablespoons coconut oil or olive oil
- 1 cup beef broth (onion free; see recipes, pages 30, 31)
- ½ cup chicken broth (onion free; optional)
- 1 tablespoon of tomato paste
- ½ medium butternut squash, peeled and cut in 1-inch cubes
- 1 small turnip, peeled and chopped in small cubes
- 2 small or 1 large carrot, chopped
- 1 green bell pepper, chopped coarsely
- 2 teaspoons thyme
- 1 bay leaf
- Dash of Celtic sea salt

Preheat oven to 325 degrees. Brown the meat in oil in a Dutch oven or large ceramic casserole. Add remaining ingredients; cover. Place in oven and cook for 3 hours. Remove bay leaf before serving.

Serves 6

Beef Kebabs

Ingredients

  1 pound beef, sirloin or boneless rib eye, cut into pieces ½-inch thick and
    1¼ inches long
  2 tablespoons olive oil, divided
  1 teaspoon turmeric
  1 red pepper, chopped in 1-inch squares
  1 yellow pepper, chopped in 1-inch squares
  1 green pepper, chopped in 1-inch squares
  1 teaspoon Celtic sea salt

In a medium-size bowl, toss meat, 1 tablespoon of olive oil, and turmeric. Let meat rest until it reaches room temperature, about 30 to 45 minutes. Thread the meat on skewers, about 5 pieces of meat per skewer. Then thread the peppers on separate skewers, about 5 or 6 pieces per skewer. Brush each skewer with the remaining olive oil and salt. Place skewers on a cookie sheet and broil for about 6 to 7 minutes, turning during the process, or cook on a hot grill for about 12 minutes or until done. Note that the veggies will cook faster than the meat, so you may want to take them off earlier.

Serves 4 to 5

Serve the kebabs on a bed of lightly sautéed baby spinach and cherry tomatoes.

Gayle Pruitt

Fast & Easy Beef Stir-fry

Ingredients

1½ tablespoons olive oil

1 pound flank steak, cut across the grain in thin strips

2 medium red bell peppers, cut in thin strips

1 cup small broccoli florets

Dash of Celtic sea salt

Add the oil to a medium–hot large skillet. Add the beef strips and cook on high for about 4 minutes. Remove steak and set aside; add vegetables and salt to the skillet and cover. Cook until vegetables are cooked through, about 3 minutes. Return the steak to the skillet and cook for another minute.

Serve with brown rice or brown rice noodles.

Serves 4

Pepper Beef with Asian Sauce

Ingredients

    2 tablespoons coconut oil

    1 pound sirloin beef, sliced in strips

    Asian Sauce (recipe follows)

    2 green bell peppers, sliced in strips

    2 yellow bell peppers, sliced in strips

    1 cup broccoli florets

    1 teaspoon fresh ginger, peeled and minced

    ¼ teaspoon ground star anise

    ¼ teaspoon ground cloves

    ½ teaspoon cinnamon

In a large skillet, heat coconut oil on medium-high heat. Brown the beef strips, turning once. Reduce the heat to medium.

Add 2 tablespoons Asian Sauce, reserving the rest to serve at the table. Cover and cook for about 15 to 20 minutes or until steak is tender. Add the remaining ingredients and cook for about 5 minutes. Cover and cook for another 5 minutes.

Serve over brown rice noodles.

Serves 4

Asian Sauce

Ingredients

    1 cup chicken broth (onion free; see recipes, pages 24, 27)

    1 tablespoon rice vinegar

    1 teaspoon sesame oil

Combine all the ingredients and mix.

3-Meat Meat Loaf

··

I use organic grass-fed meats whenever possible. This loaf is also good with ground turkey or buffalo, or use whatever meat you have on hand.

Ingredients

    ½ pound ground lamb

    ½ pound ground veal

    ½ pound ground beef

    2 medium eggs

    1 tablespoon olive oil

    1½ cups of cooked millet (recipe on page 35)

    1 stalk of celery, chopped fine

    1 yellow or green bell pepper, coarsely chopped

    1 teaspoon turmeric

    ½ teaspoon thyme

    Dash of Celtic sea salt

    1 cup tomato sauce

Preheat oven to 350 degrees. In a large bowl, add all ingredients except the tomato sauce, and mix thoroughly with your hands. Put mixture in a loaf pan and place in oven for 45 minutes or until done. Turn off the oven; pour the tomato sauce over the meat loaf and leave in the oven for an additional 5 minutes before serving.

Serves 6

Spaghetti and Meatballs

....

This recipe is also great to make in bulk. (You can double or even triple the recipe.) If you do make the bulk version, freeze the meatballs and sauce in separate containers. Make the meatballs about 1 inch in diameter. Place on cookie sheet and cook in a preheated oven at 350 degree for about 25 minutes. To serve, thaw the meatballs and the sauce in the refrigerator overnight. Add the sauce to the meatballs in a saucepan over low heat for about 10 minutes or until heated through.

You may substitute spaghetti sauce for the Red Sauce if it does not contain onions and is low in sodium.

Meatballs

Ingredients

    1 pound ground grass-fed beef

    ½ cup cooked brown rice (Chef Mimi likes to use leftover risotto)

    1 large egg or 2 small eggs

    Pinch of fennel seeds

    Pinch of dried oregano

    Dash of Celtic sea salt

    1 tablespoon extra-virgin coconut oil

Mix all the ingredients except the oil in a bowl, and form into 1-inch balls. Add the oil to a medium-hot skillet. Brown meatballs on all sides; remove from skillet and set aside.

Red Sauce

Ingredients

> 3 large red bell peppers, chopped
> 1 cup chicken or beef broth (onion and garlic free; see recipes, pages 24, 27, 30, and 31)
> 2 tablespoons tomato paste

Place all the ingredients in a food processor and purée. Place red sauce in a skillet with the browned meatballs. Cover and cook for 20 minutes on medium-low heat or until meatballs are done.

Add a small amount of toasted sesame seeds on top and serve over brown rice noodles.

Serves 4

For humans only (never canines), you can jazz it up with garlic, onion, cayenne, and a little Celtic sea salt.

Stuffed Zucchini with Beef

Ingredients

    2 large zucchini, lightly steamed (about 3 to 4 minutes)

    ½ tablespoon coconut oil

    ½ pound ground beef

    ½ bell pepper, chopped

    1 large egg

    ½ cup tomato sauce

    1 slice dry gluten-free bread, processed into bread crumbs

    ½ teaspoon oregano

    ½ teaspoon thyme

    Celtic sea salt, optional

Preheat oven to 350 degrees. Cut steamed zucchini in half lengthwise, then cut a thin slice along the bottom of each to allow the zucchini to lay flat. Scoop out the pulp to make a boat. Place pulp in cheesecloth and squeeze out excess moisture. Place zucchini boats in a glass or ceramic 1½-quart dish.

Heat oil in a skillet over medium-high heat; cook beef and peppers together until beef is no longer pink. Remove from heat and drain. Add the zucchini pulp, egg, tomato sauce, bread crumbs, and herbs to the meat. Fill the zucchini boats with the mixture. Bake uncovered in the oven for about 20 minutes.

Serves 2

Tomato Oregano Pot Roast over Spaghetti Squash

....

Pot Roast

Ingredients

    2 pounds chuck roast, cut into 1-inch cubes

    3 medium carrots

    1 tablespoon olive oil

    1 green bell pepper, cut in squares

    1 yellow bell pepper, cut in squares

    1 large can diced tomatoes (low sodium)

    1 teaspoon dried oregano

    Dash of Celtic sea salt

Add all ingredients to a large covered saucepan on medium-low heat and cook for 2 hours or until meat is fork tender.

Spaghetti Squash

Cut a medium spaghetti squash in half lengthwise. Place cut side down on a cookie sheet and bake in 350-degree oven for about 45 minutes or until squash is soft. Remove from oven and cool. Scoop out seeds from center. With a fork, shred the squash into strands. Place the shredded squash back in the shell and pour the beef over the squash for a very pretty presentation.

Serves 8

Gayle Pruitt

Chicken and Turkey Entrées

Fast & Easy Chicken Stir-fry

Ingredients

    1 tablespoon coconut oil

    1 pound chicken tenders, cut in thin strips

    1 bag of mixed frozen vegetables (no onions or corn)

    Dash of Celtic sea salt

Add oil to a large skillet and set burner to medium–high. Add chicken strips and cook for 2 minutes. Add the vegetables and salt and cook until veggies are hot.

Serves 4

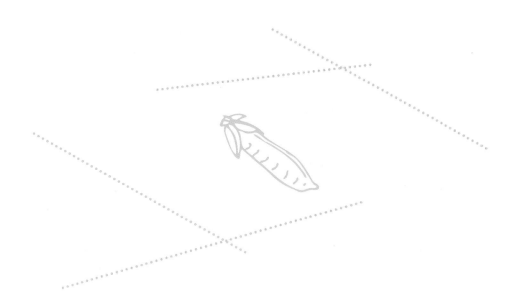

Chicken Tenders with Coconut and Sesame Seeds

....

Ingredients

　　½ cup coconut flour

　　1 tablespoon unsweetened organic shredded coconut

　　1 tablespoon raw sesame seeds

　　½ teaspoon garlic (optional)

　　½ teaspoon turmeric

　　½ teaspoon Celtic sea salt or to taste

　　2 tablespoons organic coconut oil

　　1 pound chicken tenders, sliced in strips

　　1 egg (I use organic pasture-fed), whisked

Combine the first six ingredients in a plastic bag and mix well. Heat the oil in a skillet over medium heat. Dip the chicken into the whisked egg; place in the bag, one tender at a time, and mix, shaking off excess coating. Cook the tenders in medium-hot skillet for about 5 minutes on one side and about 3 minutes on the other, or until cooked through.

Serves 4

Chicken Livers with Green Peppers

Ingredients

- 1 tablespoon coconut oil
- 1 pound chicken livers, trimmed
- 2 green bell peppers, sliced in strips
- 1 tablespoon sesame seeds
- 1 tablespoon Asian fish sauce
- 1 teaspoon chopped cilantro
- Fresh mint leaves for garnish (optional)

Add oil to a skillet and set over medium-high heat. Add livers and sauté for about 4 minutes. (They should still be pink on the inside.) Add the green peppers and sesame seeds, and cook for an additional 3 minutes. Then add fish sauce and cilantro and stir. Remove from heat.

Garnish with a few fresh mint leaves and serve over brown rice.

Serves 4

Crispy Spinach-Stuffed Chicken Breast

Ingredients

¼ cup seasoned, gluten-free bread crumbs

⅔ cup of gluten-free, Ritz-like crackers

2 teaspoons olive oil

6 cups baby spinach

½ teaspoon Celtic sea salt

4 (4- to 5-ounce) boneless, skinless chicken breasts

2 tablespoons olive oil

½ teaspoon dried thyme

1 egg, slightly beaten

Preheat oven to 375 degrees. In a food processor, blend the bread crumbs and crackers until the mixture looks like coarse cornmeal. Set aside.

Pour 2 teaspoons oil into a large skillet and set burner to medium. Add spinach and salt and cook, stirring, until the spinach begins to wilt. Remove from heat.

Use a sharp knife to cut a slit into the side of each chicken breast, being careful not to cut through. Mix together the 2 tablespoons of oil and thyme. Brush 1 tablespoon of the herb mixture into the breast cavities; stuff with spinach and press down on the breast until the pocket is closed.

Place the slightly beaten egg in one shallow pan, and the crumbs in another. Coat the stuffed chicken breasts in egg, then dredge in the crumbs.

On a cookie sheet, arrange the stuffed chicken breasts and pour the rest of the oil and herb mix over the chicken. Bake for 25 to 30 minutes.

Serves 4

Gayle Pruitt

Stuffed Chicken Breast Red & Green

Ingredients

2 large red bell peppers, roasted and split in half lengthwise
(from a jar works fine)

½ bunch of asparagus tips, cut in ½-inch pieces

1 tablespoon apple cider vinegar

2 tablespoons olive oil

2 tablespoons chopped parsley

½ teaspoon Celtic sea salt

4 chicken breasts, split, boned, and pounded

Preheat oven to 375 degrees. Lay the 4 roasted red pepper pieces flat and place 1 or 2 of the asparagus tips on the red pepper slices, and roll up.

Mix the vinegar, oil, parsley, and salt together. Lay the chicken breasts out flat and brush on the herb mixture. Put the red pepper rolls in the middle of the chicken breasts and roll up the breasts; secure with a toothpick.

Arrange the stuffed chicken breasts in a rectangular glass or ceramic baking dish. Add the remaining herb mixture and the rest of the asparagus on top of the chicken breasts. Cover with aluminum foil. Bake in oven for 25 minutes.

Serves 4

Secret Pocket-Stuffed Chicken Breast (with Uncured Turkey Bacon and Broccoli)

Ingredients

- 2 teaspoons plus 2 tablespoons olive oil
- 2 cups broccoli florets, chopped
- 1 teaspoon apple cider vinegar
- ½ teaspoon dried summer savory (or any herb you like except onion or nutmeg)
- 4 slices uncured turkey bacon, cut in half
- 4 skinless, boneless chicken breasts

Preheat oven to 375 degrees. Add 2 teaspoons of oil and the broccoli to a medium-hot skillet. Cook for 2 to 3 minutes or until broccoli turns a bright green. Mix together the remaining 2 tablespoons of oil, vinegar, and herbs; set aside.

Lay the 8 pieces of turkey bacon flat, and spoon a small amount of the cooked broccoli onto each piece. Roll the bacon up with the broccoli inside.

With a sharp knife, make a slit about 2 inches long in the fat part of each chicken breast, being careful not to cut all the way through. Brush some of the vinegar, oil, and herb mixture inside the cavity. Place 2 of the bacon broccoli wraps inside of each chicken breast. Press down on the breasts until the slit closes.

In a rectangular glass or ceramic baking dish, arrange the stuffed chicken breasts and pour the remaining oil, vinegar, and herb mixture over the chicken. Cover with aluminum foil. Bake for 25 minutes.

Serves 4

Pumpkin Seed and Lime Chicken with Spinach

Ingredients

2 tablespoons olive oil

2 ounces raw pumpkin seeds

Juice of 2 limes

Zest of 2 limes

1 teaspoon turmeric

½ teaspoon Celtic sea salt

4 chicken quarters

Add all ingredients except the chicken to a food processor and pulse until pumpkin seeds are in small chunks. Place chicken in a bowl and pour pumpkin-seed mixture over chicken, making sure to completely cover the chicken. Place in refrigerator for at least an hour.

Place chicken skin side down in a hot skillet or grill pan. Cover the chicken with a lid, pressing down on the chicken. Cook for about 10 minutes and then turn the chicken over; the skin should now be a golden brown. Turn the heat to medium–low, replace the lid over the chicken, and cook for another 30 minutes. Keep warm while preparing the spinach.

Spinach Lightly Sautéed

2 (10-ounce) bags washed baby spinach

Add spinach to the skillet that you cooked the chicken in, and sauté for about 2 minutes or until spinach is wilted. Serve chicken over a bed of spinach.

Serves 4.

Easy Tarragon Chicken Salad in Coconut Wraps

Coconut wraps are a great alternative to any gluten-type wraps. They are made from raw coconut meat and coconut water. You don't need to freeze or refrigerate them, and they are delicious. If they are not available in your area you may order online.

Easy Tarragon Chicken Salad

Ingredients

> 1 pound cooked chicken breast (you may also use dark meat),
>   cut in ¼-inch cubes
> 1 teaspoon dried tarragon or 1 tablespoon chopped fresh tarragon
> 1 tablespoon mayonnaise

Mix all the ingredients together.

Wraps

Ingredients

> 4 pure coconut wraps
> Soft lettuce leaves (such as butter lettuce)
> Roasted red peppers (I buy them in a jar and pat them dry with a
>   paper towel)
> Sprouts (I use a small amount of broccoli sprouts, optional)

Place 1 wrap on flat surface; place 1 lettuce leaf on the wrap, a slice of roasted pepper, and a small amount of the chicken mixture (and the sprouts, if desired).

Carefully roll up the wrap and repeat. Enjoy!

For large dogs, serve whole; for medium-size dogs, cut in half; for tiny dogs, cut in fourths or even eighths if the dog is very small.

Serves 4

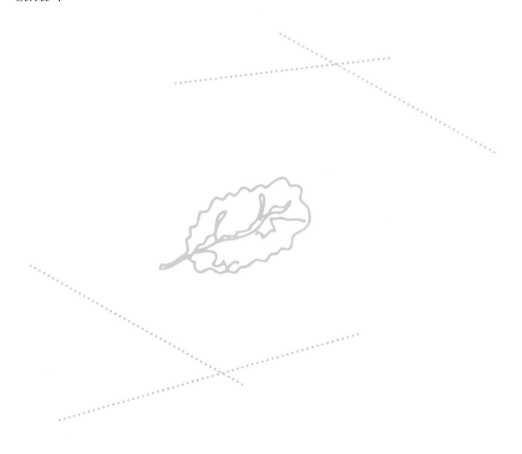

Turkey Meatballs

Ingredients

    1 pound ground turkey

    ½ cup cooked brown rice

    1 large egg or 2 small eggs

    ½ green bell pepper, diced

    2 teaspoons plus 1 tablespoon extra-virgin coconut oil

    1 pinch of fennel seeds

    1 pinch of dried oregano

    Dash of Celtic sea salt

Mix all the ingredients together in a bowl except 1 tablespoon oil. Form the mixture into 1-inch balls. Place meatballs in a glass or ceramic baking dish. Melt the remaining coconut oil and drizzle over meatballs. Cook at 325 degrees for 30 minutes or until done.

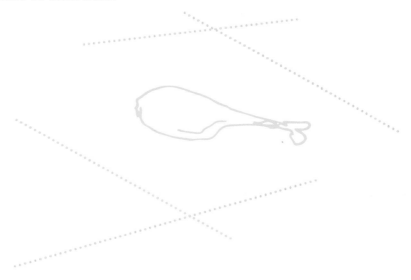

Turkey Meatloaf with Tomato Sauce

Tomato sauce:

Ingredients

    1 cup chopped fresh tomatoes

    1 teaspoon apple cider vinegar

Mix the ingredients well.

Meatloaf:

Ingredients

    1 pound ground turkey

    1 teaspoon dried basil

    1 teaspoon dried thyme

    1½ teaspoon kosher salt

    1 large or 2 small eggs

    ½ cup gluten-free bread crumbs

    1 tablespoon coconut oil

Preheat oven to 325 degrees. Combine all of the meatloaf ingredients in a large bowl and mix with your hands. Line a baking sheet with parchment paper. Form the meatloaf mixture into a loaf.

Bake the meatloaf for 30 minutes or until done. Remove from the oven and allow the loaf to rest for 10 minutes. Slice and serve with tomato sauce on the side.

Serves 4

Gayle Pruitt

Braised Turkey Thighs with Apples and Red Cabbage

Ingredients

  2 large turkey thighs

  Pinch of Celtic sea salt

  1 teaspoon turmeric

  2 teaspoons coconut oil

  4 medium-size tart apples, peeled, cored, and sliced

  2 cups purple cabbage, shredded

  Dash of cinnamon

Season the turkey with salt and turmeric. Add oil to a skillet, set over medium-high heat, and place turkey skin side down. When turkey thighs are a golden brown, about 8 to 10 minutes, turn over and add the apples, cabbage, and cinnamon. Cover and cook on medium-low heat for about 40 minutes or until the turkey meat pulls easily off the bone.

Serves 4

To serve to our canine buddies, let cool and pull turkey off bone.

Lamb
Entrées

Curried Lamb Stew

Ingredients

- 3½ pounds lamb stew meat, cubed
- 3 tablespoons coconut flour
- 3 tablespoons coconut oil
- 3 tablespoons mild curry powder
- 1 large Granny Smith apple, cored and chopped (*no apple seeds; they are toxic for dogs*)
- 1 cup chicken broth (onion free; see recipes, pages 24, 27)
- ½ cup blueberries, fresh or frozen
- Dash of Celtic sea salt

Place the lamb and coconut flour in a plastic bag and shake, coating the lamb stew meat. In a large skillet over medium-high heat, add the oil and brown the lamb. Add the rest of the ingredients; cover and cook for about an hour or until the lamb is tender.

Serves 10

Braised Lamb Shanks with Figs and Blueberries

....

You can use a leg of lamb; just cook for an additional hour.

Ingredients

    4 lamb shanks

    2 tablespoons coconut oil

    ½ small papaya, fresh or frozen (about 6 ounces), cut in chunks (optional)

    1 small yam, peeled and cut in cubes

    4 large fresh figs, cut into quarters

    1 cup blueberries

    1 tablespoon tomato paste

    1 teaspoon cinnamon

    1 teaspoon cumin

    1 teaspoon Celtic sea salt

    ½ teaspoon turmeric

    1 cup chicken broth (onion free; see recipes, pages 24, 27)

Preheat oven to 325 degrees. Brown the lamb shanks in oil in a hot skillet. Place in a ceramic or glass casserole dish and add the rest of the ingredients. Place in the oven, covered, for 3 hours.

Serves 4 to 6

Leg of Lamb

Ingredients

    1 (6 to 7 pound) leg of lamb

    1 teaspoon granulated (or powdered) garlic

    1 teaspoon cumin

    ½ teaspoon turmeric

    1 teaspoon Celtic sea salt

    2 tablespoons coconut oil

    1 small yam, peeled and cut in cubes

    4 large fresh figs, cut in quarters

    1½ cups chicken broth (onion free; see recipes, pages 24, 27)

    4 or 5 sprigs rosemary*

If your dog has a tendency for any kind of seizure, skip the rosemary. Rosemary has been known to trigger seizures in dogs that have had seizures in the past.

Preheat oven to 325 degrees.

Rub the lamb all over with garlic, cumin, turmeric, and salt. Then brown the lamb in oil in a hot skillet.

Place yam and figs in bottom of pan with chicken broth; arrange lamb on a rack with sprigs of rosemary. Place in oven. Check the lamb after 2 hours with a meat thermometer; then check every 30 minutes until inside temperature reads 165 degrees. Remove from the oven and let rest for 20 minutes before slicing.

Variation for humans only: Sauté 2 finely minced garlic cloves, $^1\!/_4$ chopped sweet onion, and 1 minced chili until the onions are transparent. Add $^1\!/_2$ cup dry red wine to the vegetables and bring to a boil. Lower the heat and simmer for 10 minutes to reduce. Strain the sauce before serving.

Serves 12 with leftovers

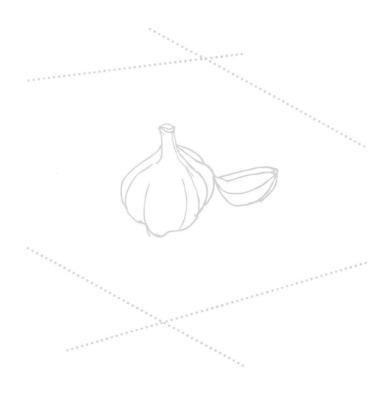

Leg of Lamb with Cumin and Bell Pepper

Ingredients

1 leg of lamb, boneless (about 3 to 4
    pounds)
1 tablespoon cumin seeds, crushed
1 tablespoon dried thyme leaves
Dash of Celtic sea salt

3 tablespoons olive oil
3 to 4 red and orange bell peppers,
    cut in thin strips
6 cups chicken or beef broth (onion free;
    see recipes, pages 24, 27, 30, 31)

With a chef's knife, punch holes all over the lamb. In a small skillet over medium-high heat, roast the herbs for about 2 minutes or until you can smell the aroma. Add salt and oil and cook for an additional 2 minutes. Cool.

Rub lamb with olive oil and herb mixture, coating uniformly (make sure some goes into the cuts in the lamb.) Cover and marinate the lamb for at least 6 hours in the refrigerator.

Preheat oven to 400 degrees. Add chicken or beef broth to bottom of roasting pan. Place lamb on a rack in the roasting pan and cook uncovered for 20 minutes. Reduce heat to 350 degrees. Place a foil tent over the lamb, add the bell pepper strips to the bottom of pan, and continue cooking for about 1½ hours or until the interior of the lamb reaches 150 degrees. Remove lamb from oven and place it on the serving platter for about 20 minutes before you slice it.

Place the roasting pan on the stove and cook over medium-high heat, reducing juices to about half. Skim fat to make a delicious sauce.

Serves 6

Lamb and Quinoa

Ingredients

- 2 pounds lamb stew meat, cut in ½-inch cubes
- 4 tablespoons olive oil, divided
- 2 cups quinoa
- 4 cups water or chicken broth (onion free, see recipes, pages 24, 27)
- 1 red bell pepper, cut in thin strips
- 1 green bell pepper, cut in thin strips
- ½ cup blanched sliced almonds
- 1 teaspoon minced ginger
- 1 teaspoon ground cardamom
- ½ teaspoon ground cloves
- 1 clove garlic, minced
- Dash of Celtic sea salt

In a large skillet, brown stew meat in 2 tablespoons of oil over medium-high heat until almost tender, about 10 minutes. Add the rest of the ingredients, cover, and simmer for 30 minutes.

Serves 8

Shepherd's Pie with Lamb

Ingredients

For the Topping

1 whole cauliflower, cut into small florets

¾ teaspoon Celtic sea salt

2 teaspoons olive oil

1 egg yolk

For the Meat Filling

2 tablespoons olive oil

1½ pounds ground lamb

1 teaspoon Celtic sea salt

1 stalk of celery, chopped fine

½ cup zucchini, sliced

½ cup broccoli, chopped

2 carrots, peeled and diced small

1 clove garlic, minced

2 teaspoons tomato paste

½ cup chicken broth (onion free; see recipes, pages 24, 27)

1 teaspoon fresh thyme leaves, chopped

⅔ cup frozen English peas, thawed

Gayle Pruitt

Preheat oven to 375 degrees.

In a saucepan, steam the cauliflower for approximately 10 to 15 minutes until fork-soft. Drain cauliflower in a colander, squeezing out excess moisture, and return it to the saucepan. Add oil and egg yolk while cauliflower is still hot and mash mixture until smooth.

While the cauliflower is steaming, prepare the filling. Place the oil into skillet and set over medium-high heat. Add the lamb and salt and cook until browned, 4 to 5 minutes. Add celery, zucchini, broccoli, and carrots and sauté an additional 4 minutes. Add the garlic and stir. Add the tomato paste, chicken broth, and thyme and mix. Simmer for about 10 minutes or until the sauce slightly thickens. Add peas to the meat filling.

Spread the meat filling evenly into a round 10-inch glass pie dish. Using a spatula, spread the mashed cauliflower over the meat filling (it may not cover the filling completely). Place the filled pie dish on a sheet pan and bake for 30 minutes or just until the cauliflower begins to brown. Let the pie cool for about 15 to 20 minutes before serving.

Serves 6

Fish Entrées

Canines are the only species susceptible to salmon poisoning, and raw salmon could cause death. Salmon (salmonid fish) or any fish that swim upstream to breed can be infected with Nanophyetus salmincola, a parasite. This parasite is harmless to almost all species except canines. So just to be safe, bake any fish that you feed your dogs to a temperature of over 300 degrees for more than 10 minutes, or sauté until fish is cooked through to be sure that you kill this particular parasite.

Pan-fried Halibut

Ingredients

   4 6-ounce halibut steaks

   ½ cup quinoa flour

   1 teaspoon turmeric

   1 teaspoon ground ginger

   2 tablespoons chopped parsley

   1 tablespoon fresh cilantro, finely chopped (optional)

Rinse the halibut steaks and pat dry. Place the quinoa flour, turmeric, and ginger in a plastic bag. Add 1 steak at a time to the bag and shake lightly.

Add oil to a large skillet over medium heat. Place the floured halibut steaks in the hot skillet (do not overcrowd) and cook about 4 minutes or until golden brown on one side. Turn and let cook for about another 2 minutes or until steak is cooked through and golden brown on both sides. Remove from the skillet and garnish with fresh herbs.

Serve with sautéed vegetables and rice or quinoa.

Serves 4

Check to make sure all fish bones have been removed when feeding canines.

Asparagus Salad with Smoked Salmon

Ingredients

- 1 pound asparagus, trimmed
- 1 tablespoon extra-virgin olive oil
- ¼ cup chicken broth (onion free; see recipes, pages 24, 27)
- 3 cups (packed) torn frisée lettuce
- 1 (6-ounce) package of smoked wild salmon

Place trimmed asparagus along with oil and chicken broth in a skillet. Turn burner to high and bring to a very slight boil. Cover and take off heat. Let sit for 4 minutes; remove lid and let cool.

On a platter, arrange frisée lettuce and cooled asparagus. Cut the salmon in strips and add to salad. Dress salad with a vinaigrette.

Serves 4

Serve with Stuffed Jeweled Eggs with salmon roe (recipe on page 120).

Asparagus and Salmon Casserole

Ingredients

    12 ounce can of salmon

    1 cup asparagus, lightly steamed

    3 ounces gluten-free bread, crumbled

    1 teaspoon paprika

    ¼ cup chopped parsley

    ¾ cup plain goat yogurt

    2 teaspoons water

Preheat oven to 350 degrees. Layer the salmon and asparagus; put bread crumbs over each layer. Top with bread crumbs and sprinkle with paprika and parsley. Mix yogurt and water; pour over the top. Bake for 35 minutes.

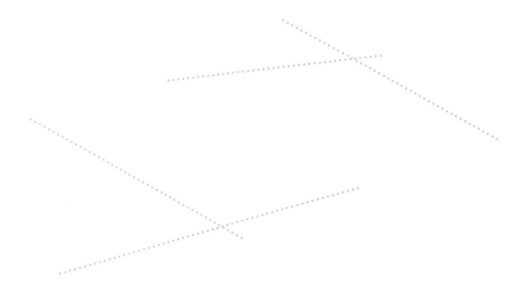

Gayle Pruitt

Poached Salmon on Bed of Chard

Ingredients

  2 cups water or vegetable broth (onion free; see recipe, page 32)

  1½ pounds salmon fillet, skin on

  5 to 6 fresh basil leaves, intact

  2 tablespoons olive oil

  ½ teaspoon Celtic sea salt

  2 bunches of chard (about 20 ounces), stemmed and chopped (save stems for salads or bulk dog food

Add liquid to a skillet and set burner to medium. Once simmering, add salmon, skin side down; cover and cook for about 8 minutes or until salmon is opaque. Uncover and remove from heat. Add fresh basil leaves and let sit. In another skillet add the oil, salt, and chard and sauté until chard is wilted. Arrange chard on platter and place salmon on top.

Serves 4 to 5

Fish Burger with Parsley Dilled Mayonnaise

Fish

Ingredients

8 ounces cod, haddock, or halibut

2 tablespoons coconut flour

Pinch of dill

Pinch of paprika

Dash of Celtic sea salt

2 tablespoons extra-virgin coconut oil

2 lettuce leaves

2 tomato slices

2 gluten-free buns

Cut fish into two 4-ounce sections. In a plastic bag, combine coconut flour, dill, paprika, and salt. Add the fish and shake gently until all the fish is coated. Put oil into skillet and heat to high. Add the coated fish and cook on each side until golden brown, about 6 minutes on one side and about 2 minutes on the other. To prepare fish burgers, spread Parsley Dilled mayonnaise on a bun bottom. Then add fish burger, lettuce and tomato, and bun top to complete.

Makes 2 fish burgers

Parsley Dilled Mayonnaise

Ingredients

    1 tablespoon mayonnaise

    1 tablespoon chopped fresh parsley

    1 teaspoon chopped fresh dill or a pinch of dried dill

Mix ingredients together and spread on buns. Build your burgers with lettuce and tomato slices (no onions!). Serve with Sweet Potato Fries. (See recipe page 106.)

Serves 2

Our "fries" are really baked. It's better not to give our best friends fried foods, though occasionally it's okay BUT only if you use coconut oil.

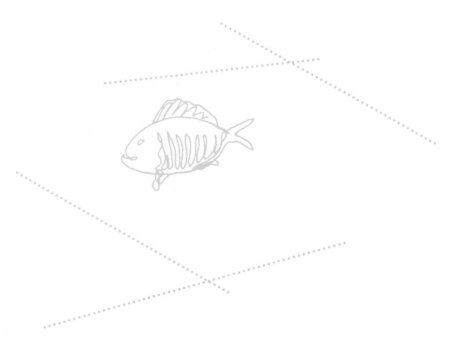

Fish Nuggets

Ingredients

  4 tablespoons quinoa flour

  1 teaspoon baking soda

  1 teaspoon turmeric

  Pinch of paprika

  Pinch of Celtic sea salt

  1 pound cod, cut in ¾-inch nuggets

  3 to 4 tablespoons coconut oil

Place first five ingredients in a plastic bag. Add cod nuggets a few at a time and gently shake. Add the oil to a large, heavy skillet and turn burner to medium-high. When oil is hot, add the nuggets a few at a time and cook until golden brown, about 3 to 4 minutes. Remove nuggets from skillet and place on paper towel. Serve with Parsley Dilled Mayonnaise (see recipe page 92) and a green salad with herbs.

Serves 4

Egg
Entrées

Pumpkin Frittata

....

Note: Do not use canned pumpkin pie filling, just pumpkin. You will need a large, nonstick oven-safe skillet for this recipe.

Ingredients

1½ cups pumpkin, fresh-cooked or canned

8 eggs

1 teaspoon water (or organic carrot juice, if you like)

1 red bell pepper, chopped in small squares

1 orange bell pepper, chopped in small squares

½ cup pitted, sliced Greek Kalamata olives that have been rinsed of excess salt
(please make sure to remove all pits from olives)

1 teaspoon summer savory (or substitute thyme or basil)

Dash of Celtic sea salt

⅛ cup olive oil *or* 2 tablespoons butter

Preheat oven to 375 degrees.

Add all of the ingredients except the oil to a bowl and whisk until thoroughly mixed. Place oil in a large, nonstick skillet and set to medium–hot. When oil is hot, add the egg mixture and cook for about 5 minutes.

Place skillet in the preheated oven for 25 to 28 minutes. Remove when eggs are completely done (no jiggling in the center). With a knife, go around the edge of the frittata, being careful not to scratch the skillet. Take the handle of the skillet and carefully turn the frittata over onto a large plate or platter. The bottom of the frittata should be a beautiful orange.

Serves 8 to 10 people or dogs; leftovers are good cold.

The canine kids will love this frittata. Great for the night before Thanksgiving or a quick easy dinner party. Simply serve with a green salad.

Gayle Pruitt

Spinach and Chard with Parsley KuKu (Classic Persian egg dish)

....

Ingredients

  1 (10-ounce) bag of spinach, chopped

  6 large chard leaves, stemmed and chopped (save stems for salads or bulk dog food)

  1 cup parsley, chopped

  2 teaspoons cilantro, chopped

  5 eggs

  1 teaspoon turmeric

  Salt to taste

  3 tablespoons olive oil

Place all ingredients except the oil in a food processor and process about 1 minute or until all vegetables are about the same size and egg is frothy. Add oil to a skillet (use a cast-iron or nontoxic, nonstick skillet) and set burner to medium-high. When oil is hot, pour the vegetable and egg mixture into skillet and spread evenly in bottom of the pan. Turn heat down to medium-low and cook for about 15 minutes.

Check the underside of mixture; if golden brown, take the handle of the skillet and gently slide mixture onto a plate, golden side down. If needed, add another tablespoon of oil to the skillet. Carefully turn plate over onto the skillet, now with the golden side up. Cook for another 10 minutes, or until cooked through.

May be served with minted or dilled yogurt, if desired (recipe follows).

Serves 4

Minted or Dilled Yogurt

Ingredients

    8-ounce container of Greek-style yogurt

    1 teaspoon mint or dill; more if you like

    Salt, to taste

Mix ingredients together and place in refrigerator until ready to use, or make the day before.

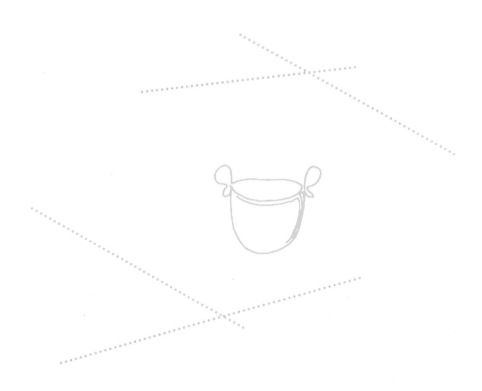

Collard Greens and Bell Pepper KuKu

Ingredients

    1 bunch collard greens, stemmed and chopped

    2 bell peppers, seeded and chopped

    1 bunch of parsley, stemmed and coarsely chopped

    5 eggs

    1 teaspoon turmeric

    ½ teaspoon salt, or to taste

    2 tablespoons olive oil

Place all ingredients except the oil in a food processor, and process for about 1 minute or until all vegetables are about the same size and egg is frothy.

Add oil to a skillet over medium-high heat. When oil is hot, pour the vegetable and egg mixture into the skillet and spread the mixture evenly across bottom of the pan. Turn heat down to medium-low and cook for about 15 minutes.

Check the underside of mixture, and if golden brown take the handle of skillet and gently slide mixture onto a plate, golden side down. If needed, add another tablespoon of oil in skillet. Carefully turn plate over on skillet with the golden side up and cook for another 10 minutes. Serve with Minted or Dill Yogurt. (See recipe on page 98.)

Serves 4

Egg Foo Yung

Ingredients

1 cup brown rice spaghetti noodles, cooked

½ cup snow pea sprouts

½ cup broccoli florets

1 tablespoon sesame seeds

¾ cup thinly sliced beef steak

1 tablespoon coconut oil

5 extra-large eggs, well-beaten

Dash of Celtic sea salt

Asian Sauce (recipe follows)

In a large bowl, mix noodles, sprouts, and broccoli thoroughly.

Toast sesame seeds for 1 to 2 minutes in a dry skillet.

Cook beef slices in hot skillet with oil for about 3 minutes. Add noodles and veggies to the skillet and stir well. Pour beaten egg over beef and noodle mixture; add sesame seeds and let cook without stirring. When egg mixture is golden brown and looks like a pancake, gently flip it over and cook until both sides are golden brown.

Asian Sauce

Ingredients

1 cup doggie chicken broth (onion free; see recipes, pages 24, 27)

1 tablespoon rice vinegar

1 teaspoon sesame oil

In a saucepan, add all ingredients and cook until hot. Spoon over pancake and sprinkle the toasted sesame seeds over the top.

Serves 4 to 5

Human/Canine
Side Dishes

Baked Sweet Potato

Preheat oven to 375 degrees. Place a large sweet potato on a lined cookie sheet and bake in oven for 45 minutes or until soft to touch. Serve when cooled.

Baked Sweet Potatoes and Apples

Ingredients

- 1 teaspoon coconut oil
- 1 large sweet potato, peeled and chopped in ½-inch cubes
- 1 Granny Smith apple, cored and chopped in ½-inch cubes (no seeds; they're toxic for dogs)
- 1 teaspoon lemon juice
- ½ teaspoon cinnamon

Preheat oven to 350 degrees. Coat a 1 half-quart glass or ceramic ovenproof dish with coconut oil. Combine remaining ingredients and place in dish. Cover and cook in preheated oven for 30 minutes.

Serves 2

Baked Sweet Potatoes with Coconut and Bananas

Ingredients

    1 teaspoon coconut oil

    1 large sweet potato, peeled and chopped into ½-inch cubes

    ½ cup unsweetened, shredded coconut

    1 banana, sliced in small coins

    1 teaspoon lemon juice

Preheat oven to 350 degrees. Coat a half-quart glass or ceramic ovenproof dish with oil. Combine remaining ingredients, place in dish, and cover. Cook in oven for 30 minutes.

Serves 2

Sweet Potato Fries

Ingredients

1 to 2 large sweet potatoes

1 tablespoon melted coconut oil

1 teaspoon paprika

Preheat oven to 400 degrees. Slice raw sweet potatoes in half, lengthwise; slice each half into ¼-inch-wide long strips, and then cut in half.

Place on a lined cookie sheet. Pour the melted oil over potatoes and sprinkle with paprika. Cook for about 15 minutes.

Serves 2 to 4

Gayle Pruitt

Brussels Sprouts with Braised Fennel

Ingredients

  1 pound Brussels sprouts, stemmed and sliced thinly

  1 fennel bulb, cut in quarters

  ½ cup chicken broth (onion free; see recipes, pages 24, 27)

  1 teaspoon coconut oil

  1 teaspoon fennel seeds (helps with digestion)

Add all the ingredients to a skillet; cover and cook on low heat for about 10 minutes.

Serves 4

Brussels Sprouts with Rosemary

Ingredients

  1 pound Brussels sprouts, stemmed and lightly steamed

  1 tablespoon olive oil

  1 teaspoon dried rosemary

Cut Brussels sprouts in half and sauté in pan with oil and rosemary until browned.

Serves 4

If your dog has had seizures in the past, skip the rosemary.

Roasted Brussels Sprouts and Cauliflower

Ingredients

½ pound Brussels sprouts, stemmed

1 cauliflower, pulled apart into florets

2 teaspoons paprika

1 tablespoon coconut oil, melted

Preheat oven to 375 degrees. Lightly steam Brussels sprouts for 5 minutes. Place Brussels sprouts and cauliflower on foil-lined cookie sheet in a single layer. Sprinkle on the paprika and pour oil over the vegetables; cook in oven for about 30 minutes.

Serves 4

Sweet Pepper Rainbow Sauté

Ingredients

    1 tablespoon olive oil

    1 red pepper, sliced lengthwise

    1 yellow pepper, sliced lengthwise

    1 orange pepper, sliced lengthwise

    1 green pepper, sliced lengthwise

    ¼ cup purple cabbage, sliced thinly

    Dash of Celtic sea salt

Add oil to skillet set over medium-high heat. Add the vegetables and salt; sauté for about 3 to 4 minutes.

Serves 4

Lightly Poached Cauliflower, Carrots, and Kale

Ingredients

    ½ cup chopped kale or collard greens

    ½ cup organic chicken broth (onion free, see recipes, pages 24, 27)

    ½ teaspoon savory or sage

    Dash of Celtic sea salt

    ½ cup thinly sliced carrots

    ¾ cup cauliflower florets

Place kale, broth, sage, and salt in pan and cook over medium heat until kale is tender, about 8 minutes. Add carrots and cauliflower and cook for an additional 4 to 5 minutes.

Serves 4

Gingered Carrots with Pears

Ingredients

    4 medium carrots, peeled and sliced thinly on the bias

    ¼ inch fresh peeled ginger root, finely chopped

    2 teaspoons coconut oil

    1 pear, peeled and thinly sliced (discard the seeds)

    Splash of white balsamic vinegar

    Celtic sea salt to taste (optional)

Sauté carrots and ginger in oil over medium-high heat until carrots are just tender. Add sliced pears and a splash of balsamic vinegar and cook 1 minute more. Add a touch of salt if desired.

Serves 4

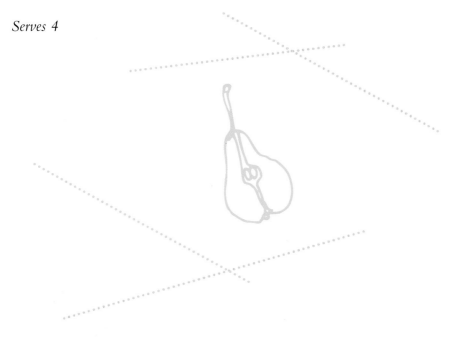

Sautéed Spinach and Cherry Tomatoes

Ingredients

    1 tablespoon olive oil

    2 (10-ounce) bags baby spinach, washed

    1 pint cherry tomatoes

    ½ teaspoon Celtic sea salt

Add oil to skillet and warm over medium-high heat. Add the spinach, tomatoes, and salt. Sauté until the spinach is just wilted.

Serves 6

Snow Peas Sesame

To trim, cut the tip of each snow pea and pull out the tough string that runs along its side.

Ingredients

    1 tablespoon coconut oil

    1 tablespoon sesame seeds

    1 pound fresh snow peas, trimmed

Heat oil in skillet over medium-high heat and add the sesame seeds; cook for about 1 minute. Add snow peas. Stir snow peas with sesame seeds and cook for about 1½ minutes.

This is an easy and delicious side dish or can be served over rice and chicken. Serves 4.

Snow Pea Salad

....

To trim, cut the tip of each snow pea and pull out the tough string that runs along its side.

Ingredients

2 quarts water

⅛ cup salt

1 pound fresh snow peas, trimmed

2 roasted red bell peppers, cut in strips

1 ounce raw pumpkin seeds

Vinaigrette

½ cup organic apple cider vinegar

⅓ cup organic extra-virgin olive oil

⅛ inch fresh ginger, finely minced

In a large saucepan, bring 2 quarts of salted water to boil; add fresh trimmed snow peas. Let boil for 1 minute. Shock the peas by plunging them into an ice bath. Be sure all peas have been submerged. When all peas are cold, about 2 minutes, drain and pat dry with a paper towel. Add peas, red pepper strips, and pumpkin seeds to a salad bowl and toss.

To make dressing, add all vinaigrette ingredients into bowl and whisk.

Serves 4

Red and White Rice with Rosemary

For special occasions such as Christmas.

Please note that when you cook rice, quinoa, and millet for canines, you should add more water and cook longer. It is much easier on their digestive system.

White Rice

Ingredients

    1 teaspoon coconut oil

    ½ cup white jasmine rice

    1¼ cups water

    Dash of Celtic sea salt

Place oil in a skillet and set over medium–high heat. Add rice and stir until rice is coated with oil. Add water and salt; cover and cook on low heat for about 25 minutes. Leave lid on rice and remove from burner.

Red Rice

Ingredients

    1 teaspoon coconut oil

    ½ cup red rice

    2 teaspoons fresh rosemary, chopped*

    1½ cups water

    Dash of Celtic sea salt

Place oil in a pan and set over medium-high heat; add rice and rosemary and stir until rice is coated with oil. Add water and salt; cover and cook on low heat for about 45 minutes. Leave lid on rice and remove from burner. Let sit for 15 minutes.

Mix white and red rice together and place on platter.

Use as a bed for a golden roast turkey or chicken. Garnish with branches of fresh rosemary.

Serves 6

* *Do not add rosemary if your dog has ever had a seizure of any kind.*

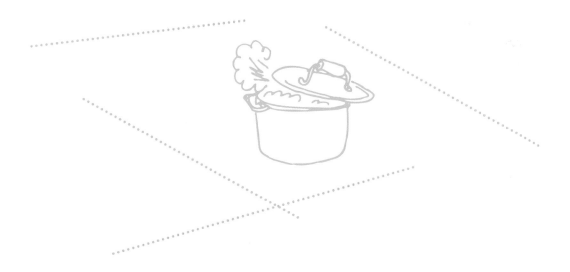

Quinoa Dressing with Cranberries

Ingredients

2 teaspoons coconut oil

1 cup quinoa

2¼ cups water or chicken broth (onion free; see recipes, pages 24, 27)

2 stalks of celery, chopped fine

½ cup dried, fresh, or frozen cranberries (Do *not* substitute cran-raisins)

Pinch of sage

Pinch of thyme

Dash of Celtic sea salt

Add oil and quinoa to a pan and set heat at medium-high. Stir until quinoa is coated with the oil. Add rest of ingredients. Turn the burner on low and let cook for about 18 minutes.

Serves 4

Stuffed Jeweled Eggs

Ingredients

    4 hard-boiled eggs, peeled

    ½ tablespoon mayonnaise

    1 teaspoon dried dill or 2 teaspoons fresh dill, chopped

    1 tablespoon wild red salmon roe

Slice eggs lengthwise and gently take out the yolk. Place yolk in a bowl; add mayonnaise and dill. Mash mixture together with a fork. Fill eggs with mixture. Divide the salmon roe into four even amounts and top each egg with it.

Serves 4

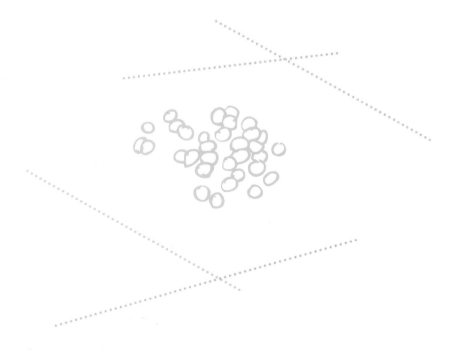

Apples and Blueberry Bake

Ingredients

    1 teaspoon coconut oil, melted

    4 cored tart apples, sliced (No seeds; they're toxic for dogs.)

    1 cup fresh blueberries

    Squeeze of lemon

    ½ teaspoon lemon zest

    ½ teaspoon cinnamon

Preheat oven to 350 degrees. Brush melted oil on the bottom of a glass or ceramic baking dish. Arrange apple slices covering the bottom of dish. Pour blueberries over the top. Squeeze lemon juice over the apples and berries. Sprinkle the lemon zest and cinnamon over the top. Cover and bake for 25 minutes.

Serves 6

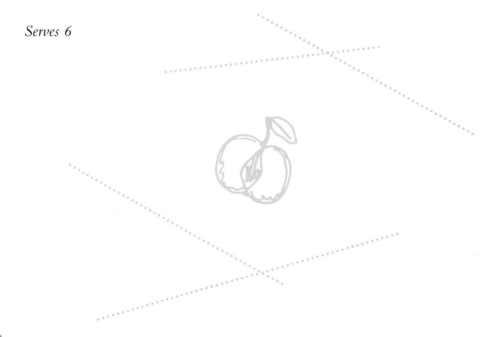

Zucchini Cakes

Ingredients

2 medium zucchini

1 to 2 teaspoons Celtic sea salt

1 egg, separated

1 teaspoon dried savory

¼ cup fresh basil, chopped

½ teaspoon baking soda

⅓ cup gluten-free, all-purpose flour

2 tablespoons coconut oil

Grate the zucchini into a colander in the sink. Add the sea salt and toss with the zucchini. Let the zucchini sit in the colander in the sink for about 10 minutes, while the salt helps to draw out the moisture. Rinse off salt completely. Place zucchini in cheesecloth and lightly squeeze to remove any excess moisture. Place zucchini on paper towel and blot gently.

Whisk the egg whites until frothy but not quite stiff.

In a medium-size bowl, add baking soda to gluten-free flour and mix. Add the grated zucchini, egg yolk, and herbs. Gently mix; then carefully fold in the egg whites.

Warm the oil in a skillet set over medium-high heat and drop heaping table-spoons of the mixture into the oil. Flatten each with a back of large spoon or spatula. You should see bubbles form and then pop around the edges. When the bubbles at the edge of the batter pop and a hole is left that does not immediately close up, flip the cake gently. Continue cooking until both sides are golden brown. Drain on paper towels.

Serve with a little unsweetened apple sauce. Serves 2.

Zucchini and Yellow Squash with Snow Peas

Ingredients

    1 teaspoon olive oil

    1 medium zucchini, thinly sliced

    1 medium yellow squash, thinly sliced

    2 ounces snow peas (about 10)

    Celtic sea salt to taste (remember you are feeding a canine so go light on the salt)

    Pinch of fresh thyme or tarragon

Add oil to a skillet and sauté zucchini, yellow squash, and snow peas for 2 to 3 minutes over medium-high heat. Add salt and fresh herbs when almost finished.

Serves 4

Zucchini, Carrots, and Red Peppers

Ingredients

    2 teaspoons olive oil

    1 zucchini, julienned

    2 medium carrots, julienned

    1 small red pepper, julienned

    ½ teaspoon thyme or your favorite herb

Add oil to a skillet and sauté all the ingredients over medium-high heat for 3 minutes.

Serves 4

Zucchini Ribbons

Ingredients

  2 teaspoons olive oil

  2 medium zucchinis, cut in ⅛-inch ribbons (I use a mandolin)

  Dash of Celtic sea salt (optional)

Add oil to a skillet and set over medium-high heat. Add zucchini ribbons and cook for about 1 minute. Roll up each zucchini ribbon, salt to taste, and place on a plate to serve immediately.

This is great with fish!

Serves 4

Canine-Only Entrées

The amount to feed your particular pooch depends on his size, breed, and metabolism. For example, Mimi and Casper each weigh about 18 pounds. I feed Mimi almost twice what I feed Casper. Mimi burns more calories by just breathing and wagging her tail than Casper does by walking a mile. So, serving size depends on your special dog. If your dog is too thin, feed him more. If your dog is gaining weight, feed him less. Common sense should prevail.

Raw

Raw Beef Supreme

....

This is a nutrient-dense meal.

Ingredients

3 small cans or 1 large can sardines, packed in water, rinsed of salt, drained

1 small sweet potato, cooked, cooled, and peeled (or substitute butternut or acorn squash, or 1 cup cooked or canned pumpkin)

2 to 3 large collard greens or kale leaves, stemmed and chopped

½ cup frozen peas, thawed

¼ tablespoon parsley

¼ cup blueberries or cranberries

1 tablespoon flax meal or sprouted flax

½ tablespoon nutritional yeast

¾ tablespoon coconut oil

½ tablespoon bonemeal (I like Now brand)

1 teaspoon fennel seeds or ½ inch fresh ginger, chopped

1 teaspoon doggie digestive enzymes (see page 181)

1 pound grass-fed beef, raw, cut into ½-inch cubes (can substitute lamb or buffalo)

Place all ingredients, except the beef, in a food processor and process until blended thoroughly. Add mixture to beef and blend thoroughly by hand.

Place mixture in individual snack bags and place those bags in freezer, always leaving one in the refrigerator. At night, take another bag out of the freezer and place in refrigerator so it is thawed by the next morning.

To be more "green," you can always buy small freezer containers that can be reused.

Makes approximately 9 (3-ounce) servings

Beef Bulk Recipe

Double or even triple this recipe and store in individual servings in the freezer.

Ingredients

   3 small cans or 1 large can of sardines, packed in water, rinsed of salt, drained

   1 large carrot, chopped

   2 large collard green leaves, stemmed and chopped

   ¼ cup frozen peas, thawed

   ¼ cup parsley, chopped

   ¼ cup frozen cranberries, thawed

   1 tablespoon flaxseed meal (I use sprouted)

   1 teaspoon eggshell calcium powder, about 1 eggshell (see Supplement chapter)

   ½ tablespoon nutritional yeast

   1 pound raw beef roast, cut in ½-inch cubes for small to medium dogs; 1-inch cubes for larger dogs

Place all ingredients, except the beef, in a food processor and process until blended thoroughly. Add mixture to beef and blend thoroughly by hand.

Makes approximately 8 (3-ounce) servings

Raw Roast and Liver Dinner

Ingredients

    3 stalks celery, chopped

    3 carrots, chopped

    1 red bell pepper, chopped

    ¾ cup frozen peas, thawed

    1 tablespoon coconut oil

    1 tablespoon nutritional yeast

    1 teaspoon turmeric powder

    2 pounds chuck roast, cut in ½-inch cubes

    6 ounces beef liver, chopped

Place all ingredients, except chuck roast and beef liver, in food processor and process until smooth. Add the mixture to the meats and blend thoroughly by hand. Place in individual containers and freeze.

Makes approximately 15 (3-ounce) servings

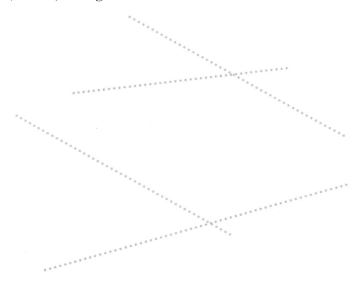

Casper's Favorite Bulk Rump Roast Dinner in the Raw

Ingredients

    2 medium carrots, chopped

    2 cups mixed salad greens (*no* iceberg and *no* onions)

    2 large collard green or kale leaves, chopped

    1 tablespoon coconut oil

    1 tablespoon chia seeds

    1 tablespoon raw pumpkin seeds

    2 teaspoons nutritional yeast

    1 teaspoon eggshell calcium for a 2-pound roast (add ½ teaspoon more if 3
        pounds)

    1 teaspoon chlorophyll

    1 teaspoon apple cider vinegar

    2 to 3 pounds raw rump roast (preferably grass- or green-fed), cut in ½-inch
        cubes

Add all ingredients, except meat, in a food processor and process until puréed.
Add a small amount of water if needed. Mix the vegetable mixture with the
cubed meat. Make individual servings and freeze.

Makes approximately 15 (3-ounce) servings

Raw Beef Heart

(Your butcher can prepare the beef heart for you. You may have to preorder it.)

Ingredients

    1 cup cabbage or collard greens, chopped

    4 stalks celery, stringed and chopped

    4 cups romaine lettuce, chopped

    ½ cup fresh parsley, chopped

    2 carrots, chopped

    1 tablespoon chia seeds

    1 tablespoon kelp powder

    2½ to 3 pounds butchered beef heart, cut in ½-inch cubes

Place all ingredients, except the beef heart, in a food processor and process until smooth. Add mixture to the meat and blend thoroughly by hand. Place in individual containers and freeze.

Makes approximately 16 (3-ounce) servings

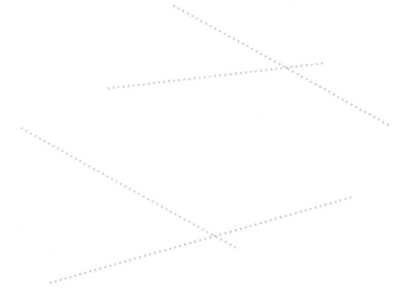

Fancy Heart Tartar

You can double, triple, or even quadruple this recipe if your furry kids are having guests.

Ingredients

⅛ teaspoon turmeric powder

¼ inch of fresh ginger root, chopped fine

3 ounces of raw beef heart, coarsely chopped

1 medium zucchini, cut ribbon-style and lightly cooked (I use a mandolin to cut very thin)

½ red bell pepper, chopped fine

1 hard-boiled egg chopped

Mix the turmeric and ginger into the chopped beef heart. Spoon beef-heart mixture into a small round mold and press down with back of spoon. (The mold should be three-quarters full. Place in refrigerator for at least 30 minutes. When it is time to serve, place the mold with the heart mixture on a serving plate and carefully unmold. Gently place the zucchini ribbon around the mold. Add some of the chopped red pepper and the chopped egg on top.

Makes approximately 2 (3-ounce) servings

Cooked Roast and Liver Dinner

Ingredients

- 2 pounds chuck roast
- 6 ounces beef liver, chopped
- 3 stalks of celery, chopped
- 3 carrots, chopped
- 1 red bell pepper, chopped
- 1 cup cooked millet
- 1 tablespoon coconut oil
- 1 teaspoon turmeric
- 1 tablespoon nutritional yeast

Preheat oven to 325 degrees. Place all ingredients except the nutritional yeast in a ceramic casserole dish and cook for about 3 hours. Let cool. Chop meat, add the yeast, and mix well. Place in individual freezer containers.

Makes approximately 14 (3-ounce) servings

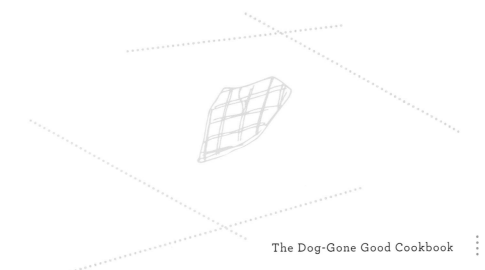

Cooked Beef Heart Dinner

Have your butcher remove the ventricles and cube the heart for you. You may have to order it in advance.

Ingredients

   2½ to 3 pounds butchered beef heart, cut in ½-inch cubes

   1 cup cabbage or collard greens, chopped

   4 stalks celery, stringed and chopped

   4 cups spinach or chard, chopped

   ½ cup chopped parsley

   1 medium sweet potato, cut in small cubes

   2 tablespoons olive oil

   2 teaspoons sage

   1 tablespoon nutritional yeast

Preheat oven to 325 degrees. Place all ingredients except the nutritional yeast in glass or ceramic casserole dish and cook for 3 hours or until heart is tender. Let cool. Add yeast, mix thoroughly, and place in individual freezer dishes.

Heart will keep for about 4 days in the refrigerator.

Makes approximately 16 (3-ounce) servings

Cooked Turkey Entrée

Double or triple this recipe and store in individual servings in the freezer.

Ingredients

½ cup cooked sweet potato

2 fresh Brussels sprouts, stemmed, lightly steamed and chopped

½ cup frozen peas, thawed

½ cup cranberries

⅛ cup pumpkin seeds

1 tablespoon coconut oil

¾ tablespoon bonemeal or eggshell calcium

1 teaspoon flaxseed

½ teaspoon sage

Dash of Celtic sea salt

1 pound cooked turkey thigh meat, chopped

Place all the ingredients except turkey meat in a food processor, and process for about 1 minute or until the mixture looks like cornmeal. Add the mixture to the turkey meat and blend by hand. Either freeze or use within two days.

When I serve this, I add a small amount of cod liver oil for pets before serving.

Makes approximately 7 (3-ounce) servings

Salmon Dinner with Braised Fennel

Ingredients

    2 fennel bulbs

    1 cup chicken broth or fish stock

    Fennel stalks and leaves, chopped

    1½ tablespoons olive oil

    1 teaspoon fennel seeds

    ½ cup parsley

    3 cans salmon, rinsed (to get rid of excess salt)

Cut each fennel bulb into quarters and braise in 1 cup of either chicken or fish stock for 15 minutes or until just tender. Place the oil, braised fennel, raw fennel stalks and leaves, seeds, and parsley in food processor and purée. Add the fennel mixture to the salmon and combine thoroughly by hand. Freeze in individual containers.

Makes approximately 11 (3-ounce) servings

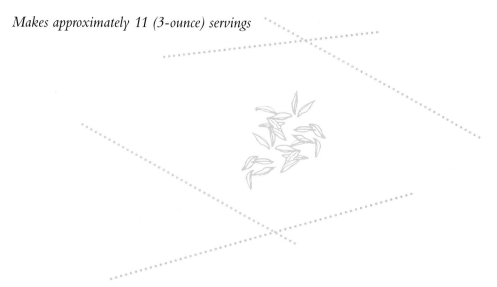

Sardines and Salmon Dinner

Ingredients

    4 (3¼ ounce) cans of sardines packed in spring water, rinsed (to get rid of excess salt)

    1 can salmon packed in water, rinsed (to get rid of salt)

    1 large sweet potato, cooked and peeled

    1 tablespoon coconut oil

    2 heads cooked celeriac (celery root), mashed

    1 teaspoon fresh dill, chopped

Mix all ingredients together thoroughly. Place in serving size containers and freeze.

Makes approximately 7 (3-ounce) servings

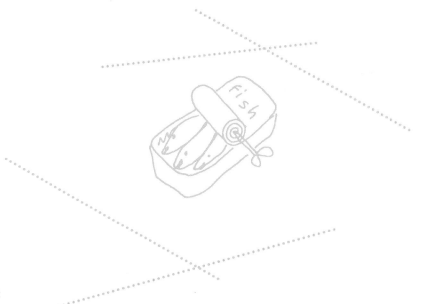

Cod and Sweet Potato Dinner

Lakewood Veggie Juice is the only brand I've found with no onion, available in local health food stores. Also, you can make your own using vegetables from the "good" vegetables list in the front of the book.

Ingredients

1½ pounds cod

2 teaspoons coconut oil

1 cup low-sodium Lakewood Veggie Juice

1 cooked sweet potato, cut in cubes

½ cup fresh parsley

1 teaspoon fresh dill, chopped

1 teaspoon turmeric

Add the cod, coconut oil, and the veggie juice to a skillet, and cook over medium-high heat for about 8 minutes, or until done. Mash cod with a fork. In a food processor, add sweet potato, parsley, dill, and turmeric and process until smooth. Add the mixture to the mashed cod and blend thoroughly by hand. Place in individual containers and freeze.

Makes approximately 12 (3-ounce) servings

Vegan

This section includes a couple of vegan bulk recipes that you can serve fresh or freeze, and some nutritional supplement suggestions that may help the vegan dog stay healthy. Because of the way our canine kids' digestive systems are designed, I do not recommend a totally vegan diet. However, if you do decide to feed your dog a completely plant-based diet, I do have some suggestions, which can be found here and in the Supplements chapter. For example, dogs need higher levels of protein than humans, and it is difficult to get these high amounts from plants. Not only is it difficult to make sure they are getting the right *amount* of protein but it also needs to be the *right kind* of protein.

They also need amino acids for their heart—such as L-Carnitine and taurine—that only come from meat. L-Carnitine and taurine deficiency can cause serious heart disease in your best buddy. When your dog is on a vegan diet, supplementation of these aminos is essential, but please investigate the source of L-Carnitine and taurine.

There are synthetic L-Carnitine and taurine amino acids that you can buy, but avoid the cheap toxic products, which can be dangerous. Check out the source; avoid the DL-Carnitine. You can find a vegetarian calcium carbonate that will be acceptable for the vegan dog.

By all means please use a complete digestive enzyme for dogs such as probiotics, and plant omega-3 fatty acids chia and flax seeds.

Our dogs have a difficult time digesting grains and legumes. They do not have any amylase in their mouths, like humans, to start the digestive process. So, when using rice or quinoa (quinoa is not a grain; it is a seed) or any legume (beans), please cook them until they are completely soft. Use more water or liquid than most recipes call for and cook 10 to 20 minutes longer than normal. This will help the dog's ability to digest and absorb the nutrients.

Red Lentil and Quinoa Deluxe

....

Ingredients

    4 quarts water or vegetable broth (onion free; see recipe, page 32)

    3 cups red lentils

    1 cup quinoa

    1 red bell pepper

    ½ pound green beans, lightly cooked

    2 cups cooked butternut squash

    1½ tablespoons coconut oil or olive oil

    1 tablespoon nutritional yeast

    1 teaspoon fennel seeds

    2 teaspoons calcium carbonate

Pour liquid into a large pot and turn burner to medium. Add the lentils and quinoa, and cook for 1 hour (add more liquid if needed). When cool, add all the ingredients to a food processor and purée. You may need to process in batches. Place in individual containers and freeze.

Divide into four containers; freeze three and keep one in the refrigerator. It will keep for one week.

Green Lentils with Brown Rice & Kombu

Soak your green lentils with a strip of kombu (a sea vegetable), available at any health food store. Lentils contain oligosaccharides, making legumes hard to digest, and kombu actually contains the enzyme needed to break down the oligosaccharides.

I have not found any studies of canine diets using kombu, but one of the many minerals in kombu is vanadium, which appears to play a multifaceted role in the regulation of carbohydrate metabolism and blood sugar. This mineral may help to regulate your dog's blood sugar when going vegetarian.

Ingredients

- 3 cups green lentils
- 1 strip kombu
- 5 quarts water or vegetable broth (onion free, see recipe, page 32) plus 5 cups of water
- 2 cups brown rice
- 4 to 5 stalks asparagus
- ¼ cup parsley, chopped
- 1 cup frozen green peas, thawed
- 1 cup shredded romaine lettuce
- 3 carrots, chopped
- ¼ cup snow peas or broccoli sprouts
- 2 tablespoons coconut oil
- 1½ tablespoons nutritional yeast
- 2 teaspoons dill weed
- 2½ teaspoons calcium carbonate

Soak lentils with 1 strip of kombu for at least 3 hours, or overnight. To begin cooking, rinse the lentils. Then add 5 quarts of liquid to a large pot, and turn burner to medium. Add the lentils and kombu and cook for 1½ hours. Add more liquid if needed. Cool.

Cook the rice in 5 cups of water for 1½ hours. Add all of the ingredients to a food processor and purée. (You may need to purée in batches). Divide into 4 or 5 containers and freeze, keeping one in the refrigerator. It will keep for 1 week.

Gelatins

Gelatins have many wonderful benefits, and the biggest one of all is that dogs love them.

When you use my chicken or boney beef broth, the health benefits triple. Homemade broth is rich in calcium, magnesium, and other trace minerals. The minerals in broth are easily absorbed by the body. Bone broth even contains glucosamine and chondroitin.

In addition to all that wholesomeness, gelatins are also fairly low in phosphorous and high in liquid, which make them perfect for the chronic renal failure diet.

The various vegetables I use and their pigments add antioxidants, anthocyanins, and carotenoids that help keep humans as well as your canines healthy and happy.

You may dilute with ½ cup of water to lower the phosphorus content.

Beef Gelatin protein: The gelatin is rich in the amino acids found in collagen, including L-proline, L-hydroxyproline, and glycine. It contains no fat, cholesterol, or carbohydrates, is free of any additives, and is easy to digest.

Chlorophyll: When you add chlorophyll to your gelatin, they make a mighty duo. Chlorophyll may help to detoxify the body and work in the digestive tract, keeping an agreeable environment for our mutt's friendly bacteria. Chlorophyll may also help to break down calcium oxalate stones so that the body can eliminate them more easily. And besides that, your furry little buddy's breath will smell much nicer.

Wiggly Beef Red Hearts

Ingredients

    3 red bell peppers, puréed

    2 tablespoons water

    3 to 4 ice cubes

    4 Knox gelatin envelopes

    3 cups hot doggie beef broth (onion free; see recipes, pages 24, 27)

Purée the red bell pepper and water; pour into a bowl and add the ice cubes. Sprinkle gelatin over the top of the purée; stir and let stand for 2 minutes. Add hot broth to the mixture and stir until the gelatin has dissolved, about 5 minutes. Place in a flat glass container and refrigerate until firm, about 3 hours. To serve, cut in squares or use a heart-shaped cookie cutter.

Makes approximately 4 cups of gelatin

Optional: Place thin round carrot slices on the bottom of the container so each serving will include a carrot slice.

Wiggly Chicky Green Stars

Ingredients

⅛ cup parsley, chopped

⅛ cup asparagus, chopped

1 teaspoon liquid chlorophyll

3 to 4 ice cubes

4 Knox gelatin envelopes

1 quart hot doggie chicken broth (onion free; see recipes, pages 24, 27)

Purée the parsley, asparagus, and chlorophyll; pour into a bowl and add the ice cubes. Sprinkle gelatin over the top of the purée; stir and let stand for 2 minutes. Add hot broth to the mixture and stir until gelatin has completely dissolved, about 5 minutes. Place in flat glass container and refrigerate until firm, about 3 hours.

To serve, cut in squares or use a star-shaped cookie cutter.

Optional: Place sweet red pepper slices on the bottom of the flat glass container so each serving will include a slice of sweet red pepper.

Makes a little over 1 quart of gelatin

Asparagus Green Gelatin

Ingredients

    1 bunch asparagus (about 10 stalks), chopped and lightly steamed

    1 cup water

    2 ice cubes

    5 Knox gelatin envelopes

    1 quart chicken broth (onion free; see recipes, pages 24, 27)

Purée asparagus in a food processor (add a little water if necessary). Pour into a small bowl and add ice cubes. Sprinkle in the gelatin and stir; let sit for 2 minutes.

Heat the broth until almost to a boil. Add the gelatin mixture to the broth and stir for a few minutes until all the gelatin has dissolved. Pour mixture into a flat-bottom glass dish and refrigerate. Cut in cubes or use a cookie cutter if your canine kids are having guests.

For smoother gelatin, juice the asparagus and only use the juice. Use the pulp in the bulk food recipes.

Makes a little over 1 quart of gelatin

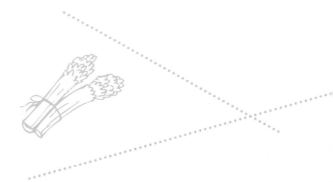

Yellow Gelatin

Ingredients

    3 yellow bell peppers, chopped

    1 yellow summer squash

    1 cup water

    2 ice cubes

    5 Knox gelatin envelopes

    1 quart chicken broth (onion free; see recipes, pages 24, 27)

Purée bell peppers and squash in a food processor. Add a little water if necessary.

Pour into a small bowl, add ice cubes, and sprinkle in the gelatin. Stir and let sit for 2 minutes.

Heat the broth until almost to a boil. Add the gelatin mixture to the broth and stir for a few minutes until all the gelatin has dissolved.

Pour mixture into a flat-bottom glass dish and refrigerate. Cut in cubes or use a cookie cutter if your canine kids are entertaining.

For smoother gelatin, juice the vegetables and only use the juice. Use the pulp in the bulk food.

Makes a little over 1 quart of gelatin

Carrot Gelatin

Ingredients

    2 ice cubes

    1 cup carrot juice

    5 Knox gelatin envelopes

    1 quart chicken, beef, or bone broth (onion free; see recipes, pages 24, 27, 30, 31)

Place ice cubes and carrot juice in a bowl and sprinkle the gelatin over the juice. Let stand for 2 or 3 minutes.

In a saucepan, bring broth to a boil; remove from heat. Pour carrot and gelatin mixture into hot broth and stir for about 5 minutes, until gelatin is completely dissolved. Pour mixture in a flat-bottom glass dish and place in refrigerator.

Options: stir ½ cup of cooked sweet potato, pumpkin, or green peas into mixture.

Makes a little over 1 quart of gelatin

Cranberry Gelatin

Ingredients

    1 cup fresh or frozen cranberries, thawed and mashed

    ½ cup water

    2 ice cubes

    5 envelopes Knox gelatin

    1 quart chicken, beef, or bone broth (onion free; see recipes, pages 24, 27, 30, 31)

Purée cranberries and water in a food processor or blender. Pour into a bowl with ice cubes. Sprinkle the gelatin over the cranberry purée; let sit for 2 or 3 minutes.

In a saucepan, bring broth to a boil; remove from heat. Pour gelatin mixture into hot broth and stir for about 5 minutes until gelatin is completely dissolved. Pour mixture in a flat-bottom glass dish and place in refrigerator.

Makes a little over 1 quart of gelatin

Vegan Gelatin

Ingredients

    1 quart Lakewood Super Veggie juice (only veggie juice without onion)

    1 ounce or 8 teaspoons of powdered agar-agar seaweed*

Special note for agar-agar: Serve sparingly because it may cause loose bowels. For a small dog (20 pounds or less), serve one 1-inch cube per day; use two 1-inch cubes for a medium dog (30 to 50 pounds) and three 1-inch cubes for dogs over 50 pounds.

Heat veggie juice on medium-hot burner; remove from heat and stir in agar-agar. Pour into a flat-bottom glass dish and refrigerate.

Variations: Stir ½ cup of cooked sweet potato, pumpkin, or green peas into mixture.

Makes about a quart of gelatin

Sauces

Veggies Plus!

Sometimes it's impractical to make all your pet's food from scratch, so if you're feeding your furry baby a good commercial-brand dog food and want to introduce some fresh, raw, or lightly cooked vegetables, this section is for you.

For the beginner, you may start out with a cooked or raw vegetable sauce to pour over the commercial food. To start, use 1 teaspoon for small to medium dogs and 1 tablespoon for larger dogs. After you make the sauces, freeze them in individual servings. Just take them out of the freezer the night before and spoon on to their regular dog food. They will last in the refrigerator about 4 days. They're fresh and wholesome and your dog will love them.

I have many sauces listed here because I believe so strongly in variety. Your dog—like you—gets bored with the same old food day after day. So I say MIX IT UP! It's good for you and good for your dog.

Herbs are another much overlooked ingredient that helps with digestion and has a myriad of other uses. Fennel, ginger, and turmeric have been used for thousands of years. They taste great, are inexpensive, and are excellent for digestion. Just a small amount is all that is needed for these superstars:

- Fennel seeds, bulbs, and leaves—Fennel is good for digestion, reducing gas and bloating, and has been used for infants' colic and for pain. Place the seeds in a coffee grinder and grind them into a fine powder or purée in a food processor with other vegetables. The fennel bulb may be used raw or lightly braised and the raw leaves can be puréed in the food processor.
- Ginger—use either dried, ground, or the fresh roots. Finely mince or purée

the raw root. Ginger is known for its digestive properties, for nausea, and for inflammation.

- Turmeric—helps with digestion and is an anti–inflammatory. It has been used successfully for pain, arthritis, and to help protect the liver. Turmeric is called the poor man's saffron because it turns food a beautiful orange or yellow.

In addition to the sauces, you may add any of the following to commercial dog food and any sauce before serving:

- 1 teaspoon of apple cider vinegar
- ½ teaspoon of ground flax or chia seeds

Cooked Sauces

Cooked Sauce # 1:
Butternut Squash & Peppers

Ingredients

    1 cup cooked butternut squash

    1 cup chopped red or orange bell pepper, lightly sautéed

    ¾ cup water

    1 teaspoon turmeric

    1 teaspoon ground ginger

    ½ tablespoon olive oil

Place all ingredients in a food processor and purée until smooth. Place in individual serving bags and freeze until ready to use.

Makes approximately 22 ounces

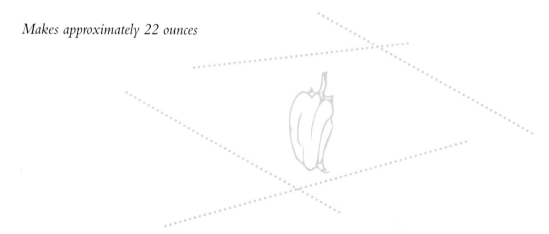

Cooked Sauce # 2:
Pumpkin & Cranberries

Ingredients

　1 cup cooked or canned pumpkin

　½ cup organic fresh or frozen cranberries

　½ cup slightly steamed fennel or celery

　¾ cup water

　½ teaspoon cinnamon

　½ teaspoon ginger

　1 teaspoon turmeric

Place all ingredients in a food processor and purée until smooth. Place in individual serving bags and freeze until ready to use.

Makes approximately 22 ounces

Cooked Sauce #3: Green Beans & Asparagus

Ingredients

    1 cup slightly steamed green beans

    1 cup slightly steamed asparagus

    ½ cup slightly steamed broccoli

    ½ cup water

    1 teaspoon fennel seeds

Place all ingredients in a food processor and purée until smooth. Place in individual serving bags and freeze until ready to use.

Makes approximately 24 ounces

   Gayle Pruitt

Cooked Sauce #4: Orange Sauce

Ingredients

    1 large cooked sweet potato

    1 cooked acorn squash

    1½ cups carrot juice (juice your own or buy pure carrot juice)

    1 teaspoon turmeric

    ½ teaspoon cumin

Place all ingredients in a food processor and purée until smooth. Pour into jar or freezer containers and freeze. When serving, spoon over dog food.

Makes about 22 ounces

Cooked Sauce #5: Yellow Sauce

Ingredients

    3 medium yellow summer squash, sliced and lightly steamed

    1 cup cooked butternut squash

    1 cup carrot juice (juice your own or buy pure carrot juice)

    1 teaspoon turmeric

    ½ teaspoon cumin

Place all ingredients in a food processor and purée until smooth. Pour into jar or freezer containers and freeze. When serving, spoon over dog food.

Makes approximately 22 ounces

Raw Sauces

Raw Sauce #1: Puréed Broccoli, Peas, and Spinach Sauce

Ingredients

¼ cup broccoli florets, either raw or lightly steamed

⅛ cup broccoli sprouts, raw or lightly steamed (optional)

¼ cup frozen peas, thawed

2 cups baby spinach leaves loosely packed, raw or lightly steamed

½ cup chicken broth (onion free; see recipes, pages 24, 27)

¼ teaspoon fennel seeds

Pinch Celtic sea salt

Place all ingredients in a food processor and purée until smooth. Pour into a jar or freezer container and freeze. (This sauce will freeze well.) Great sauce to spoon over meat, eggs, or chicken.

Makes approximately 12 ounces

Raw Sauce #2: Green Fennel Sauce

Ingredients

    3 fennel bulbs, leaves and stalks, chopped

    2 cups filtered water

    2 teaspoons chlorophyll

    1 teaspoon fennel seeds

Place all ingredients in a food processor and purée until smooth. Pour into jar or freezer containers and freeze. When serving, spoon over dog food. Fennel has been used to help with digestion for thousands of years.

Makes approximately 22 ounces

Raw Sauce #3: Red Sauce

Ingredients

    3 to 4 large red bell peppers

    1 tablespoon low–sodium tomato paste

    2 stalks celery, chopped

    1 cup water, or more

    1 teaspoon paprika

    1 teaspoon turmeric

Place all ingredients in a food processor and purée until smooth. Pour into jar or freezer containers and freeze. When serving, spoon over dog food.

Makes approximately 12 ounces

Raw Sauce #4: Fresh Green Salad Sauce

Ingredients

    2 medium cucumbers, peeled and sliced

    1 whole head romaine lettuce, chopped

    2 medium zucchini, sliced

    2 teaspoons chlorophyll

    1 teaspoon celery seeds

Place all ingredients in a food processor and purée. Pour into a jar or freezer container and freeze. When serving, spoon over dog food.

Makes approximately 12 ounces

Raw Sauce #5: Peas & Spinach

Ingredients

    1 cup frozen peas, thawed

    1 cup washed baby spinach

    ½ cup water

    ½ tablespoon olive oil

    1 tablespoon parsley

Place all ingredients in a food processor and purée until smooth. Place in individual serving bags and freeze until ready to use.

Makes approximately 20 ounces

Raw Sauce #6: Fennel & Romaine

....

Ingredients

    1 cup fennel stalks and leaves

    1 cup romaine lettuce

    1 tablespoon fresh dill

    ½ tablespoon olive oil

    1 cup water

Place all ingredients in a food processor and purée until smooth. Place in individual serving bags and freeze until ready to use.

Makes approximately 14 ounces

Raw Sauce # 7: Cranberries, Celery, & Carrots

....

Ingredients

    1 cup fresh organic cranberries   1 cup water

    ½ cup chopped celery   1 teaspoon chlorophyll

    ½ cup chopped carrots

Place all ingredients in a food processor and purée until smooth. Place in individual serving bags and freeze until ready to use.

Makes approximately 18 ounces

Raw Sauce #8: Green Peas & Carrots

Ingredients

    1 cup green peas, thawed

    1 small raw carrot, chopped

    1 cup water

    ¼ teaspoon fresh ginger, chopped

Place all the ingredients in a blender or food processor and purée until smooth. Place in individual serving bags and freeze until ready to use.

Makes approximately 15 ounces

Raw Sauce #9: Broccoli & Parsley

Ingredients

    1 cup raw broccoli

    ¼ cup parsley

    1½ cups water

    1 red bell pepper

    1 yellow bell pepper

    ½ teaspoon turmeric

Place all the ingredients in a blender or food processor and purée until smooth. Place in individual serving bags and freeze until ready to use.

Makes approximately 20 ounces

Gayle Pruitt

Raw Sauce #10:
Butternut Squash & Spinach

Ingredients

    1 cup cooked butternut or acorn squash (or pumpkin or sweet potato)

    2 cups raw spinach

    1½ cups water

    ½ teaspoon fennel seeds

Place all the ingredients in a blender or food processor and purée until smooth. Place in individual serving bags and freeze until ready to use.

Makes approximately 18 ounces

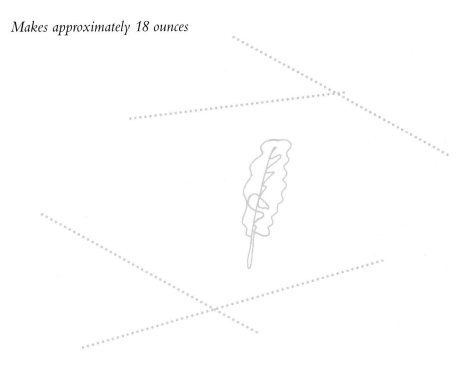

Snacks & Treats

Instead of giving your adorable pooch some store-bought, fat-laden, overcooked treat from a possibly suspicious source, why not give that canine kid a carrot?

"A carrot!" you say.

I have heard so many people tell me their dogs would never touch a carrot. Well, they would if you dipped that bit of nutritious vegetable in some yummy beef broth. This works not only with carrots but with bell peppers, bits of summer squash, or even a small amount of cooked sweet potato.

Some fruits also make great treats. Give your pal a little sliced apple, a tiny bit of banana with some raw almond butter, or some fresh ripe blueberries.

I also give my canine kids helpings of gelatins as treats. All I have to do is say, "Does anybody want some jelly?" and they will jump over each other to eat that wiggly piece of tasty nutrition. (Only use plain gelatin with your own veggies and broth.)

Here are a few treats. Some are especially good on hot summer days!

Frozen Blueberries with Almond Butter

Ingredients

    ½ jar almond butter

    1 pint fresh organic blueberries, washed

Line a cookie sheet with wax paper. Place several rows of almond butter mounds (a little more than a teaspoon) on the cookie sheet, making sure that the dollops are not touching. Place several blueberries in the center of each mound. Place in freezer.

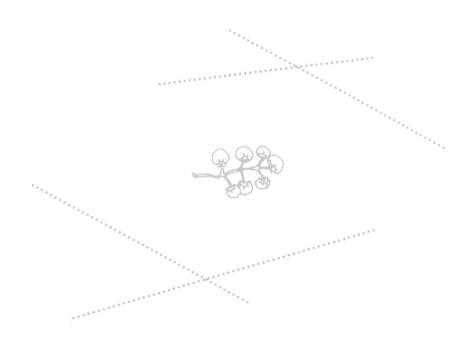

FRUITS
CONFITS
GELÉE

Veggie Popsicles

Pick one of the sauce recipes (see pages 162 to 171), and instead of placing in a large container, pour the sauce in an ice tray and freeze. Your little guys will love these little cubes of frozen Veggie Popsicles.

Sweet Potato Dollops

Ingredients

    1 sweet potato, cooked

    ½ teaspoon cinnamon

    2 tablespoons Greek-style yogurt

Mash sweet potato in a bowl, then add the cinnamon and Greek-style yogurt. Mix together. Give each dog 1 tablespoon or a dollop. You may sprinkle a few raspberries on top to make it even more special.

Cranberry/Blueberry Muffins

Ingredients

- 1½ cups gluten-free all-purpose flour
- 1 cup quick-cooking oats
- 1 teaspoon baking powder (aluminum free)
- 1 teaspoon baking soda
- ½ teaspoon ground cinnamon
- 2 eggs, lightly beaten
- 1 cup (8 ounces) plain goat yogurt
- ¼ cup melted coconut oil, plus 1 tablespoon
- ½ cup fresh or frozen blueberries
- ½ cup fresh or frozen cranberries

Preheat oven to 375 degrees. In a large bowl, combine the first five ingredients. Combine the eggs, yogurt, and ¼ cup of coconut oil; stir into dry ingredients until just moistened. Fold in cranberries and blueberries.

Coat muffin cups with the tablespoon of melted coconut oil; fill each cup two-thirds full with batter. Bake for 25 minutes or until a toothpick inserted in the center of a muffin comes out clean. Cool for a few minutes. Remove from pan and place on a wire rack. Serve warm with butter.

Makes 12 muffins

Suggested Supplementation

Because of the way our food is grown, shipped, stored, and cooked, our food doesn't have the same amount of nutrients as it did in the past. No matter how careful we are with our food and how we treat it, we still may need supplements to make sure that we humans and our dogs are getting all the nutrients our bodies require.

I always recommend organic, grass- and pasture-fed foods whenever possible. Not only are you getting higher quality nutrition eating this way, but you can taste the difference. Don't think your kids, canine or human, won't be able to tell the difference—they will.

Digestion and the absorption and uptake of nutrients are so important. So that's where we will begin.

This is for the canine kids. With any kind of supplementations be sure to check with your vet regarding dosage and any special requirements your dog might have.

Probiotics—friendly bacteria that reside in the gut and help your body absorb nutrients. Actually, there are many tasks that this garden of flora performs but we will just address the absorption task for now.

Even though there are no studies with Dr. Ohhira's Probiotics and canines, these probiotics are some of the best I've found and they work beautifully with all animals, humans included. There are many other good products on the market but I'm more familiar with Dr. Ohhira's.

Doggie Digestive Enzymes—help break down fat, protein, and carbohydrates. Be sure to buy a complete spectrum and not just a proteolytic enzyme that only breaks down protein. You will need to make sure the one you buy has amylase as well as lipase to break down carbohydrates as well as fats.

Apple Cider Vinegar—1 tablespoon per 1 pound of food aids digestion.

Omega-3-Fish Oil—**Do not** use cod liver oil that is for humans, which has too much vitamins A and D and can be toxic. You may use small amounts of omega-3 fish oil for humans. The liquid is better; that way you can smell the oil. If there is a strong fishy smell, it is rancid and should be thrown away. Use it on the days you are not serving fish.

Multivitamin & Minerals—talk with your vet.

Calcium—My very favorite is to make my own with eggshells for me and my dogs. I use only organic pasture-fed eggs. When I break an egg for cooking, I wash the shell and let it dry. When I have collected about a dozen shells, I make eggshell calcium.

Did you know one eggshell makes about 1 teaspoon of powder, which is around 1,000 mg or 1 gram? And to top that, it's fairly low in phosphorous and has 27 other elements including magnesium, boron, copper, sulphur, and zinc. Also, the eggshell contains hyaluronic acid and chondroitin sulfate—great for you and your dog's joints.

You can buy the supplement if you want, but by making the powder yourself you know what eggs were used. Remember, the better the eggs the higher in minerals.

How to Make Eggshell Calcium

12 washed and dried eggshells

Place eggshells in a food processor or coffee grinder (I use a coffee grinder) and grind to a fine powder. Place in a sealed jar or bag and keep dry.

Adult dogs need about 1 teaspoon (800 to 1,000 mg) of calcium per pound of dog food.

Special Note for Vegan-Fed Dogs

Your dog needs calcium. You can find calcium carbonate that will be acceptable for the Vegan Dog.

L-Carnitine and taurine deficiency cause heart disease, and the only place to obtain these amino acids naturally is from meat. And the most concentrated of these aminos are in the heart muscle tissue. When your dog is on a vegan diet supplementation of these aminos is essential. You must supplement, but please investigate the source of L-Carnitine and taurine before you give them to your precious dogs. You want the pure L-Carnitine, not the DL-Carnitine that is much cheaper to make and very dangerous.

Suggested Web Sites and Blogs

These are my favorite Web sites about health for humans and canines.

www.doggonegoodblog.wordpress.com
Mimi's and Casper's blog on the healthy, happy dog.

www.petcarenaturally.com
Dr. Shawn Messonnier's Web site.

http://drpescatore.com/blog/4
Dr. Fred Pescatore's blog on health and nutrition.

www.drohhiraprobiotics.com
Dr. Ohhira's is my favorite probiotic for humans and dogs.

www.radiomartie.com
A radio show called *Healthy by Nature* and a great resource on nutrition and the politics of health.

The Last Word

⬤ ⋯⋯⋯⋯⋯⋯⋯⋯⋯⋯⋯⋯⋯⋯⋯⋯⋯⋯⋯⋯⋯⋯⋯⋯⋯⋯⋯⋯⋯⋯⋯⋯⋯⋯⋯⋯⋯ ⬤

Humans and dogs are not that different when it comes to nutrition. And when it comes to personality, no matter how ornery some may appear, our canine friends tend to be far more loving, forgiving, caring, and loyal than we can ever be.

When Gayle approached me to write the last chapter for this book, I was very excited. I have a strong background in nutritional medicine and consistently use nutrition as the foundation for treating my patients, so why don't we take the same approach with our pets?

The amount of money, or should I say the paltry sums of money, we spend on feeding our pets is appalling. This was particularly apparent in 2007 during the wheat gluten scare that caused many pet deaths in the United States, resulting from melamine-contaminated wheat gluten and rice protein exported from China. When you look at the ingredients found in many of the most popular brands of pet food, you'll find most of them contain wheat gluten!

Really! I ask you, why are pets even expected to eat gluten or wheat for that matter? Take it one step further—these pets are carnivores who have always been considered to be hunters and gatherers. What do hunters and gatherers typically eat? They eat proteins and also a small amount of vegetables and fruits. This is the same diet that I think everyone should be eating, but let's stick to canines for the sake of this discussion.

Like most of you, I have been under the thrall of the pet food companies. I believed that what they were putting in their food was what my pet should be eating. I felt they certainly knew better than I did. After all, I studied humans, not animals. Yes, I have had pets my entire life and I fed all of them a combination of inexpensive dry and wet food from packages and cans, thinking that if I could add warm water and get the best of both worlds it was even better.

It wasn't until I received my current dog, Remington, that I was forced to learn more about pet nutrition. I rescued the most adorable beagle, and no, he doesn't howl except when we are in the country and he is in hot pursuit of deer, wild turkeys, birds, or a fox. Unfortunately, my precious new dog just kept having diarrhea no matter what brand of food he was fed. He was only three-and-a-half years old and this was at the time when all the dry, organic foods were on the market. Being in the industry, I kept switching him from one type of food to another and yet he still had diarrhea. Now I want to tell you, diarrhea in a pet is never fun. So, living in an apartment in New York City, surrounded only by pavement with no easy access to any grass for my pet, plus having to work long hours, was making my life miserable.

I finally had a brilliant idea to feed him the way he was meant to be fed by applying the knowledge about nutrition I use when I counsel humans. And guess what? The diarrhea went away immediately and it has never returned, except on rare instances when he eats something on the street that I can't get out of his mouth in time. Now his treats are raw carrots and he will do anything for one of those.

So, when Gayle told me about her book, I was thrilled. I have turned so many people on to feeding their pets this way—all with the same great success stories. It was certainly time for someone to write about it so people would not only have the ability to help their most cherished relations in the same way they can help themselves, but so they can make sure their best canine friends will live a longer and healthier life.

I know you want your pets to live forever just like I do. You also want them to feel the best they can, even though you know they won't ever complain. In this book, Gayle has given you a tool making it quite possible for you to find the same success I did. I hope you have enjoyed the book as much as I have.

—FRED PESCATORE, MD, MPH, CCN

Index